BRANDS™

A Marketing Game

BRANDS™

A Marketing Game

Randall G. Chapman

Boston University

Prentice Hall

Englewood Cliffs, New Jersey 07632

Editorial production/supervision: *Kris Ann E. Cappelluti*
Pre-press buyer: *Trudy Pisciotti*
Manufacturing buyer: *Patrice Fraccio*
Supplement acquisitions editor: *Lisamarie Brassini*
Acquisitions editor: *Sandy Steiner*

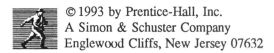
Printed in the United States of America

10 9 8 7 6 5 4 3 2

ISBN 0-13-087404-3

Prentice-Hall International (UK) Limited, *London*
Prentice-Hall of Australia Pty. Limited, *Sydney*
Prentice-Hall Canada Inc. *Toronto*
Prentice-Hall Hispanoamericana, S.A., *Mexico*
Prentice-Hall of India Private Limited, *New Delhi*
Prentice-Hall of Japan, Inc., *Tokyo*
Simon & Schuster Asia Pte. Ltd., *Singapore*
Editora Prentice-Hall do Brasil, Ltda., *Rio de Janeiro*

CONTENTS

List of Exhibits

List of Forms

List of Tables

Preface

BRANDS™ is a sophisticated marketing simulation game designed to be used on MS-DOS personal computers. Designed for use in the first marketing course (either the undergraduate marketing principles course or the first-year MBA marketing management course), BRANDS™ reflects the complexities, uncertainties, and challenges inherent in the marketing decision-making and analysis process. BRANDS™ is meant to represent "reality" to the participants, rather than simply being a "game." Nevertheless, it does represent an approximation to the real world, as do all marketing simulation games. Suggestions for ways in which BRANDS™ might be enriched would be welcome.

This marketing simulation game's name, BRANDS™, reflects its orientation: management of a number of individual brands within an organization's product line. As it is traditionally viewed, the marketing management process involves on-going marketing, competitive, and financial analysis. These efforts lead to the development of marketing strategies which are implemented within short- and long-term marketing plans. All of these marketing management elements — marketing analysis, marketing planning, and marketing strategy — arise in BRANDS™.

Linda Edwards (Boston University), Matt Elbeck (SUNY Brockport), Tom Kinnear (University of Michigan), Tom Madden (University of South Carolina), Chris Puto (University of Arizona), Al Shocker (University of Minnesota), Joe Urbany (University of South Carolina), Jim Wiley (University of Alberta), Greg Wood (Canisius College), and John Zych (University of Scranton) provided helpful advice on the final shaping of BRANDS™. Their suggestions are most gratefully acknowledged. Future revisions to BRANDS™ will inevitably be based on users' suggestions and comments. Please do pass your suggestions and comments on to the author.

Chapter 1

BRANDS™ and Marketing Simulation Games

Introduction

BRANDS™ is a marketing simulation exercise. Competing firms within a single industry make marketing decisions (price, product design, advertising, promotion, and sales force) and a simulated marketplace responds to those decisions. Marketing simulations introduce explicit competition and continuity into the learning process. Participants make decisions in response to, and in light of, likely actions and reactions of competitors. Participants must live with the results and the consequences of their decisions. Market feedback (sales, revenues, market shares, and profits) provides various degrees of positive and negative reinforcement to enhance the learning experience. Rapid and continuous feedback serves as a powerful device to generate interest and motivate participants.

The establishment of teams to handle decision making in simulation games provides another valuable learning experience. Whether the team structure adopted is line or staff or some combination, the group decision-making experience is invariably both interesting and educational. Another important feature of simulation games is their capability for compressing the time dimension. This time compression enables teams to see the outcomes of their decisions without the long waiting period that occurs in real life.

Simulation exercises are normally very enjoyable activities for the participants. Participants generally find that their interest in the game increases with the passing of each simulated decision period. The game-related decision-making process becomes an adventure rather than the tedious chore that traditional assignments and cases may become.

Some Considerations in Simulation Game Design

In constructing marketing simulation games, game designers must cope with a variety of important trade-offs. All game developers have to resolve the inherent conflicts between realism and simplicity. Of course, all simulation games must have face validity if they are to be taken seriously by the participants. Based on extensive experience with BRANDS™, participants do find it to be a challenging and realistic marketing exercise. Some of the principal marketing simulation game design considerations, and how they apply in BRANDS™, are described in Table 1.

Table 1

SOME GENERAL MARKETING SIMULATION GAME DESIGN
CONSIDERATIONS AND HOW THEY APPLY IN BRANDS™

Marketing Simulation Game Design Consideration	BRANDS™ Application/Implementation
Whether to construct the game around a specific industry or product/service, or to deal with hypothetical scenarios.	BRANDS™ is built around an unidentified durable good, vaporware, initially being sold for a few hundred dollars per unit. Vaporware is used in both industrial and consumer settings. For reference purposes, you might wish to think of vaporware as being some kind of electronic product, furniture, clothing, or mechanical product.
Whether to use single or multiple products.	Firms in BRANDS™ may market two different vaporware brands. These brands are distinguished by their physical composition of five underlying raw materials (Syntech, Plumbo, Glomp, Trimicro, and Fralange) plus Compatibility and Warranty. Firms control the composition of their vaporware brands, and can produce and market a wide range of formulations to attempt to meet customers' needs.
Whether to use single or multiple markets.	In BRANDS™, there are three regional markets ("U.S.A.," "Europe," and "Pacific").
Whether the game should be designed for conflict and competition or require the players to compete against nature.	In BRANDS™, a maximum of nine firms compete within an industry. To accommodate more than nine firms, parallel industries may be running simultaneously. However, such parallel industries are completely unrelated to each other.
Whether to encourage individual or group decision-making.	Teams in BRANDS™ are completely responsible for the management of their firms' activities. Teams may organize themselves in any way they wish to manage their affairs.
Whether to have an underlying market model that is deterministic or stochastic.	As in life, there are undoubtedly some random events in BRANDS™. Remember the cynic who said, "Sometimes you get the elevator, sometimes you get the shaft." However, extensive experience with BRANDS™ indicates that careful and thoughtful analysis, planning, and strategizing will inevitably be successful in the long run.

Decision-Making Logistics in Computerized Simulation Exercises

BRANDS™ is similar to other computerized simulation exercises with regard to the logistics associated with making decisions and receiving results. The general logistics in computerized simulation games include:

1	Teams meet and make decisions for the next decision period. Typically, some decision forms are used to record the decisions. These forms are ultimately passed on to a game administrator. (The game administrator may be the course instructor. If not, the course instructor will identify the game administrator.) The course instructor will also describe any other special procedures and requirements associated with submitting decisions.
2	The game administrator arranges to: (i) input all decisions to the game data base; (ii) run the game; (iii) generate the necessary financial and operating reports; and, (iv) assemble the reports for the teams.
3	The game administrator returns the financial and operating reports to the teams, prior to the next scheduled decision period.

The only additional consideration in BRANDS™ is that requests for marketing research studies must be made prior to the next decision period. These marketing research requests must be included along with other decision change forms submitted to the game administrator. This simulates the real world where there is a time lag between ordering marketing research and receiving marketing research results.

Management, Organization Design, and Teamwork in BRANDS™

BRANDS™ participants work in groups. Each group is assigned to manage a BRANDS™ firm. Based on experience, deliberate and thoughtful management of the talents and resources of the individual group members — by the group members themselves — is the key to success in BRANDS™.

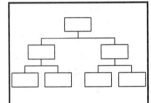

A variety of line and staff functions exist within BRANDS™. Firms must make decisions on how best to allocate their members' time to the necessary management tasks. As time passes, the initial allocation of group members to tasks may not be the best one in the light of new information and changing competitive circumstances. Teams should anticipate the need to periodically review their management structure and the allocation of their members' time to various BRANDS™ tasks.

The key point here is that management of BRANDS™ activities must be thought about regularly. Good management does not happen by chance. Experience indicates that poor (or completely absent) management is one of the major causes of poor performance in BRANDS™. Fostering high quality teamwork in your group functioning will be an important part of your team's management efforts.

Some past BRANDS™ firms have used a matrix organizational structure. In such an organization arrangement, individual team members have both line and staff responsibilities simultaneously.

An area of management which must be carefully considered concerns whether a firm will have a formally designated general manager. In the past, most smaller-sized teams (three to four members) have not adopted such an organizational structure. However, some larger-sized teams (five or more members) have opted for a formally-designed general manager position.

With regard to responsibility allocations, the following piece of advice comes from a previous BRANDS™ participant: *"Don't Take Management Responsibilities Lightly: Friends are friends and business is business. Management is the key to this game. Without effective management, you are lost. Structure your management team as a business with formal authority and delegation of responsibilities."*

Based on experience, the following key questions about group functioning are of paramount importance within the BRANDS™ exercise: How will the group be managed? Who will manage the group? How will the work be divided? How will coordination be achieved? How will work quality be ensured? How will conflicts among individuals be kept at a healthy level (not too high or low)? How often will group functioning be reviewed? Address these questions early and often within your group!

Some General Advice About BRANDS™

Attitude and perspective are important when participating in a complicated marketing exercise like BRANDS™. With regard to general attitude and perspective, the following piece of advice comes from a previous BRANDS™ participant: *"Don't treat this simulation as a game; treat it as real. This is the closest thing you can get to the real thing. Consider the profits as real and your time as a valuable commodity. Treat this game seriously; it is a chance to play the market without taking substantial financial and career risks, with the exception of personal pride!"*

Some pieces of advice about how the BRANDS™ marketplace operates are sprinkled throughout this manual. More generally, though, it is important to remember that you are in a competitive world. As one previous BRANDS™ participant put it: *"Do not underestimate your competition. Your performance will be influenced by your competitors' actions. This marketplace is sensitive to changes and movements by your competitors!"* It is important to remember that you may be able to learn about how the vaporware market works by watching closely your competitors' marketing initiatives, successes, and failures.

Welcome to BRANDS™. Have fun and take it seriously. But, attempt to learn as you go along.

The BRANDS™ Participant's Manual

The remainder of this BRANDS™ participant's manual is organized into the following chapters:
- Chapter 2 provides an overview of the BRANDS™ marketing simulation game.
- Chapter 3 includes a detailed description of all of the marketing decision variables (product design, pricing, and marketing support spending) in operation in BRANDS™.
- Chapter 4 focuses on non-marketing decision variables and product-related costs.
- BRANDS™ marketing research capabilities are described in Chapter 5. There are 20 marketing research studies that BRANDS™ firms may order. Of course, these marketing research studies have various costs associated with them.
- The various financial and operating reports that BRANDS™ teams receive after each game run are described in Chapter 6.
- Chapter 7 is devoted to performance evaluation considerations in BRANDS™.
- The BRANDS™ decision change forms and marketing research pre-order request forms are contained in Chapter 8.

The course instructor may include optional material described in Chapter 9 in your BRANDS™ exercise.
- Chapter 9 contains information about using the BRANDS™ software (program B_INPUT) to change your decision variables and pre-order marketing research studies.

Experience suggests that BRANDS™ participants refer regularly to this manual throughout the BRANDS™ marketing simulation exercise. Start off by skimming through the complete manual. Then, review Chapters 3-6 carefully and in detail. Browse through other parts of the manual as appropriate. Finally, don't feel shy about turning back to the manual regularly. There is much detail to absorb in a relatively short period of time. No one gets it all right the first time! Take heart, though. Many others have successfully completed the BRANDS™ experience. You can too!

Chapter 2

BRANDS™ Overview

Introduction

BRANDS™ is a multi-brand, multi-market marketing simulation game cast within the context of an oligopolistic industry. A BRANDS™ industry consists of a maximum of nine firms. Each BRANDS™ firm markets a variety of brands in the three BRANDS™ market regions. Firms are required to develop long-run strategies and short-term tactics, and to implement such tactics and strategies in BRANDS™.

BRANDS™ is a marketing game. Decisions required in BRANDS™ are those which normally would fall within the realm of marketing decision making. Other functions such as accounting, finance, and operations management are performed automatically within BRANDS™. Of course, BRANDS™ players must know how to interpret and analyze financial and operating statements. BRANDS™ focuses on the role of marketing planning, the development and implementation of marketing strategy, the role of financial analysis, the cost/benefit trade-offs associated with the use of marketing research information, sales forecasting, and the impacts of competitive dynamics, rivalry, and environmental forces within the context of the marketing management decision-making process.

BRANDS™ is designed to help the participants strengthen their marketing analysis, decision-making, and planning skills. BRANDS™ provides a laboratory setting in which marketing plans and strategies are formulated and executed.

The major challenge facing each firm is to attempt to sort through the maze of possible marketing decisions in each quarter and to develop "reasonable" decisions, where "reasonable" is judged in terms of the firm's long-run goals and relative to the performance of other firms in the industry. One particularly interesting feature of BRANDS™ is its extensive marketing research capabilities. Firms have the opportunity to purchase a wide range of marketing research studies. These studies should allow the members of a thoughtful firm to sort their way through the maze of the BRANDS™ world in a satisfactory manner.

The key to success in BRANDS™ is a carefully developed long-run strategy, with appropriate expertise being applied to sales forecasting, market monitoring, financial analysis, planning, and marketing decision making. Common sense and managerial acumen will be needed as well.

BRANDS™ Terminology

Some terminology is used throughout this BRANDS™ participant's manual:

- In BRANDS™, the terms "product" and "brand" are used interchangedly.
- The term "region" refers to one of the three BRANDS™ markets ("U.S.A.," "Europe," and "Pacific").
- A "game period" is a quarter, with four "game periods" (quarters) in a BRANDS™ year.

The Product Category

In BRANDS™, the product category of interest is vaporware. Vaporware is an abstract product construct that represents a wide range of durable and capital goods. Vaporware brands are initially (when the game begins) sold for a few hundred dollars per unit. Vaporware has potential for use in both industrial and consumer settings. For reference purposes, you might wish to think of vaporware as some kind of electronic or mechanical product, furniture, or possibly even clothing.

Each BRANDS™ firm may market two different vaporware brands. Vaporware brands are distinguished by their physical composition of five underlying raw materials (Syntech, Plumbo, Glomp, Trimicro, and Fralange) plus Compatibility and Warranty. Firms control their brand composition, and can produce and market a wide range of possible formulations to attempt to meet customers' needs.

BRANDS™ focuses on an abstract product, vaporware, rather than any specific existing product category so that marketing decision-making and analysis skills are emphasized. BRANDS™ participants have to learn the marketing milieu within which vaporware functions, without reference to any particular existing product category. Ad hoc marketing rules of thumb that you might have learned in connection with the marketing of various products (such as spending a certain percentage of sales revenues on advertising) may or may not work well in BRANDS™. Since BRANDS™ uses an abstract product, you will have to learn about vaporware by careful analysis, monitoring, experimentation, and the judicious use of marketing research studies. This "sink or swim" situation is just what you would have to cope with if you suddenly assumed marketing management responsibilities for some new product or service with which you were completely unfamiliar and for which there was no storehouse of brand, category, or industry knowledge, experience, expertise, or folklore. In any event, all teams are in the same situation.

Even though vaporware is an abstract product, you will find that the market for vaporware operates in a regular and sensible fashion, consistent with generally-accepted marketing and economic principles. For example, if you lower a brand's price (holding everything else constant), then sales volume will tend to increase. However, be forewarned: BRANDS™ is based on a sophisticated model of a marketplace. For example, prices that are substantially below the industry norm may lead customers to doubt the quality level of the brand, thus possibly reducing demand. Further details about such sophisticated features of the BRANDS™ world are sprinkled throughout this manual. Many things, however, will have to be discovered within the play of the game.

Vaporware appeals widely to industrial and consumer buyers. Vaporware has been around for many years and would generally be considered to be in the mature phase of the product life cycle. Over the years, the physical characteristics and composition of vaporware have changed in response to changes in customer tastes and preferences, and to technological advancements.

The Vaporware Industry

Your firm is one of the large companies in the vaporware industry. Each company in the vaporware industry is a large organization with many different product lines, one of which is vaporware. Due to various trade restrictions, tariff protection, and proprietary technology, competition from outside the vaporware industry is nonexistent.

Your Firm

Your company is divisionalized along product category lines, with each product group being a separate profit center. For various legal reasons, your vaporware division is a separately incorporated entity. Your stock trades on the stock exchange. Your corporate holding company currently controls about 50% of all of the outstanding stock of your vaporware division.

Your company and its vaporware division have both been profitable in the past. The general goals specified for your vaporware division include maintaining and improving the long-run profitability and market position of the vaporware division.

Within the vaporware division of your company, your management team has complete and total responsibility for all marketing-related functions. These responsibilities include such areas as pricing, advertising, product design, and sales force management. You will also have the opportunity to purchase various pieces of marketing research information that may assist you in making sound marketing decisions and formulating appropriate marketing strategies. Personnel, accounting, operations, and finance functions are performed at the corporate level (for which a corporate administrative overhead fee is levied against your vaporware division). Your vaporware division does not have to worry about these kinds of non-marketing activities of your firm.

Your company has a single plant which operates as a separate profit center and which produces vaporware brands for you. This plant is located in the United States. Current company policy dictates that you may buy vaporware only from your company's plant. This plant also purchases and stores raw materials for use in vaporware manufacturing. The plant has warehouse space in which finished goods are stored until shipped to dealers in the various market regions.

Market Demand Patterns

The demand for any vaporware brand depends on overall demand for the product category and the allocation of that demand into individual market shares of the competing brands. With regard to product category (industry) demand, seasonal forces do not appear to exist in the vaporware marketplace.

Market size (that is, population and GNP) and the decisions of the firms in the industry are thought to be major forces influencing overall industry demand for vaporware. For example, it has been noted in the past that heavy advertising by all firms in the industry tends to expand overall demand for the vaporware product class. Similarly, industry price levels influence overall industry demand for vaporware in the usual inverse fashion: higher industry price levels are associated with lower overall industry demand. As with all products, there are some customers who are relatively heavy users of vaporware, while others would never use vaporware even if it was free.

Market shares are influenced by the relative levels of the various marketing mix decision variables associated with each brand. Customers of vaporware seem to make implicit trade-offs among the brand offerings in terms of product design characteristics, price, and product quality. Customers are also influenced in varying degrees by firms' communications efforts in support of their brands. After all, an unknown brand is unlikely to have substantial sales! Sales force activities are directed at dealers who do seem to be influenced in varying degrees by the attention of a firm's sales force.

Experience suggests that customers' perceptions and beliefs about vaporware brands as well as actual marketing programs associated with vaporware brands influence brand choices. In particular, past research has shown that customers' perceptions of product performance and product convenience are major factors in the brand selection process.

Vaporware has an international clientele. At the present time, the three market regions in the vaporware industry are: the United States, Europe, and the Pacific (Japan, China, Hong Kong, Korea, Singapore, and Malaysia). Each of these BRANDS™ market regions may respond somewhat differently to the various marketing variables at the disposal of the firms. Thus, what might work very well in one market region could be a disaster in another market region. Each market region may well have to be viewed as a separate market segment. The three market regions in BRANDS™, along with some relevant current market statistics (as of quarter 1), are described in Table 2.

Table 2

BRANDS™ REGIONAL MARKET STRUCTURE AND SOME MARKET STATISTICS

		Population		Per Capita Income		Consumer Price Index	
	Region	Current Size	Annual Growth Rate	Current Value	Annual Growth Rate	Current Value	Annual Growth Rate
1	U.S.A.	251,000,000	2.0%	$15,510	3.5%	900	4.5%
2	Europe	230,000,000	3.0%	$14,780	4.0%	975	3.5%
3	Pacific	317,000,000	3.5%	$12,187	5.0%	950	3.0%

Note: All growth rates are estimates, as of quarter 1. These growth rates may, of course, change through time.

Currency Conventions in BRANDS™

Although vaporware is marketed internationally, all currency transactions are expressed in U.S. dollar terms. As appropriate, these currency values are translated into and from local currencies automatically within BRANDS™. Thus, for all practical purposes,   everything is denominated in U.S. dollars in all BRANDS™ decision and reports. This currency convention facilitates BRANDS™ decision making and BRANDS™ report processing, since only a single currency is involved.

Marketing Research Information

The specific details of the available marketing research studies in BRANDS™ are described in Chapter 5 of this BRANDS™ participant's manual. You have many possible marketing research studies from which to choose. These studies help you analyze the markets that you face and the competitive activities of your rivals. These marketing research studies parallel the kinds of marketing research that can be purchased and that are often used (and abused!) by marketing analysts and decision makers in the real world.

All marketing research information in BRANDS™ is supplied exclusively. That is, the marketing research information that you purchase is only for your eyes. There is no secondary resale market for marketing research information in BRANDS™. Evidence of secondary reselling of marketing research information might well lead to a termination of access to the BRANDS™ marketing research supplier for an offending firm.

You may only use information about the BRANDS™ world that you purchase through the BRANDS™ marketing research program or from the course instructor. Since the precise BRANDS™ market is not identified, you are not able to use secondary sources to determine, for example, population or GNP growth rates of BRANDS™ market regions.

Team Organization and Functioning

The exact organization and allocation of responsibilities of your team depend on the particular abilities and interests of the individual team members. Through time, and as experience with BRANDS™ is gained, reallocations of initial responsibilities may be appropriate.

Particular competitive situations and strategic initiatives may suggest the need for reallocations of short- or long-term responsibility assignments. The nature of the formal group operating structure that you adopt is not important as long as it provides for a workable and equitable assignment of responsibilities.

Based on experience, most teams in this marketing simulation game allocate responsibilities among team members in a brand- or product-management style of operation based on regional breakdowns. In such a management structure, specific individuals have responsibilities for managing the activities of all brands marketed in a specific BRANDS™ market region. This is done to capitalize on the potential regional diversity within BRANDS™. This is, of course, in contrast to a traditional product-management style of operation where a single manager would be responsible for an individual brand in all market regions where it is marketed.

Disclosure of Information, Security, and Anti-Competitive Behavior

Information about your operating practices could be very valuable to your competitors. Protect yourself!

The normal laws governing anti-trust and anti-competitive behavior are in effect in BRANDS™. Any peculiarities of BRANDS™-specific laws are indicated, where appropriate, within this documentation. For example, overt discussion of your marketing plans and policies with your industry competitors, either singly or in industry conferences, is illegal. Further, anti-competitive behavior such as price-fixing is also illegal.

The Starting Position Scenario: Quarter 1

At the beginning of quarter 1 of BRANDS™, teams take over management responsibilities of an existing division. All of the previous division executives were at a Vaporware Industry Trade Association convention and they tragically perished in a flash explosion and fire at the convention hotel. Thus, there is no one to consult with about your division's affairs. Perhaps even more unfortunately, the previous management was not noted for their record-keeping abilities, so you also have no documentation about past activities and events in the division, in the markets in which your division operates, or about the industry as a whole (beyond the information contained in this manual).

You are, however, inheriting an on-going division with on-going decisions already in place. *Whether these current marketing decisions are good, bad, or mediocre is unknown.* You will have to live with considerable uncertainty at the beginning of the BRANDS™ exercise. You have a virtually unlimited mandate to spend money in support of marketing research efforts, marketing efforts in general, and new product introduction in particular. However, you are expected to learn quickly and to improve the long-run profitability of your division.

Firm Decision Variables

In each quarter, firms must make a range of decisions. These decisions may be grouped into two categories. First, *marketing decisions* along the full range of marketing mix decision variables (product design, price, dealer rebates, advertising, promotion, sales force management, and product quality levels) will form the primary focus of each team's attention. These decisions are described in Chapter 3. The second area of regular decision-making involves *marketing research decisions*. Marketing research orders can be issued to your firm's marketing research supplier requesting specific marketing research studies to be conducted. Chapter 5 describes the marketing research studies which are available in BRANDS™.

BRANDS™ has a special continuous decision framework built into it. All decisions from the previous quarter carry-over intact into the present quarter, unless a firm issues orders to change a decision. All firm decisions in BRANDS™ are, therefore, standing decisions and they continue to be in force until explicitly changed by a firm. Note, however, that the ordering of marketing research studies must be done in every quarter in which such studies are required.

You submit your decision change and marketing research requests at designated times. Your decision changes are entered into the BRANDS™ data base prior to the next game run. Your marketing research is conducted after the next game run; its results are returned to you along with the usual set of BRANDS™ financial and operating statements.

Chapter 3

Marketing Decision Variables

Introduction

In this chapter of the BRANDS™ participant's manual, the full range of marketing decision variables currently in operation in BRANDS™ is described in detail. These marketing variables are extensive, and they allow a wide variety of marketing programs to be initiated and sustained. A range of marketing program possibilities exists in BRANDS™ so that teams may seek to establish decisive sustainable differential advantage.

The BRANDS™ marketing program variables include:

- product design
- price
- research and development activity
- advertising (amount and media copy content)
- promotion
- sales force management (size, allocation, and compensation program)
- sales forecasting.

Dollar spending allocations (via advertising, promotion, and sales force activities) are a major way in which each firm provides marketing support to its brands.

Product Design Decisions

Vaporware is composed of five basic raw materials: Syntech, Plumbo, Glomp, Trimicro, and Fralange. Three pounds of raw materials are required to make one unit of standard vaporware. The specific combinations of Syntech, Plumbo, Glomp, Trimicro, and Fralange to make vaporware are at the control of each firm. The specific mix of raw materials determines the type of vaporware manufactured and marketed. The composition of vaporware is determined by the percentage allocations (by weight) of the five basic raw materials that constitute vaporware. In standard vaporware, these percentages sum to 100% (and, naturally, none of the percentages can be negative).

Vaporware is composed of combinations of these five raw materials, with percentage compositions being at least 1% and no more than 99% for each of the five raw materials. (Other technological limits — described below — must also be met.) Vaporware also may be manufactured with varying levels of Compatibility (vaporware product attribute #6) and Warranty (vaporware product attribute #7). The Compatibility and Warranty dimensions are both on "1" to "9" scales. A "1" on the Compatibility scale represents vaporware that has very little compatibility with other existing vaporware products, while a "9" describes vaporware that is highly industry-compatible with other existing vaporware products. The Warranty scale is expressed in months. For example, a score of "5" on Warranty indicates that you offer a five-month warranty on a vaporware brand. As described in Chapter 4, selection of Compatibility and Warranty levels can dramatically influence the costs associated with vaporware manufacturing.

In summary, vaporware brands are described by the seven product attributes (or characteristics) of:

> Syntech composition (% of weight)
> Plumbo composition (% of weight)
> Glomp composition (% of weight)
> Trimicro composition (% of weight)
> Fralange composition (% of weight)
> Compatibility score (1-9 scale)
> Warranty score (1-9 scale).

Various vaporware brands are described by their particular configuration of these seven dimensions.

Within the vaporware industry, specific brands of vaporware are described by their mix of raw materials and their positioning on Compatibility and Warranty. For example, a 40/15/35/ 5/ 5/3/7 vaporware brand is composed of 40% Syntech, 15% Plumbo, 35% Glomp, 5% Trimicro, and 5% Fralange with a positioning of "3" on the Compatibility dimension and a positioning of "7" on the Warranty dimension.

The terms "formulation" and "composition" are used interchangeably within BRANDS™ to denote the particular configuration of a vaporware brand on these seven underlying product dimensions.

Each BRANDS™ firm may have a maximum of two different vaporware brands. Within BRANDS™, these are described in terms of "firm#-brand#" notation. Thus, vaporware brand 3-2 is the terminology used to describe the second brand of firm #3 in a vaporware industry.

A specific formulation of a vaporware brand is the same in all market regions. Thus, brand formulation is product-specific, not product- and market-specific. Therefore, the formulation of brand 4-1 (firm 4, brand 1) is the same in all BRANDS™ market regions. It is not possible to have one formulation of brand 4-1 in BRANDS™ region 1 and another formulation of brand 4-1 when it is marketed in BRANDS™ region 3. The formulation of brand 4-1 is always the same in all market regions.

There is no legal constraint in BRANDS™ prohibiting copying competitors' vaporware brand formulations.

Vaporware Technology Constraints

Current vaporware technology constraints limit formulation possibilities. Specifically, the following two technological constraints exist in the vaporware industry:

- The raw material content of the first five vaporware product attributes must sum to exactly 100. This corresponds to exactly three pounds of raw materials input.
- The fourth and fifth vaporware product attributes — Trimicro and Fralange — must each be equal to exactly 5.

These two vaporware technology constraints together imply that the first three vaporware product attributes (Syntech, Plumbo, and Glomp) must sum to exactly 90, corresponding to 2.7 pounds of raw materials.

Reformulation Decisions

Firms have full discretion and control over the formulations of their vaporware brands, subject to existing vaporware technology constraints. Through time, firms may wish to reformulate their brands, perhaps to adjust to changing customer preferences or to respond to changing costs of raw materials. A reformulation is defined as a change in any or all of a vaporware brand's seven attributes (Syntech, Plumbo, Glomp, Trimicro, Fralange, Compatibility, and Warranty). Thus, even a change as small as one unit on a single vaporware attribute is considered to be a complete reformulation.

Your research and development group and your plant manager have jointly concluded that costs of $500,000 are incurred for any reformulation of an existing brand of vaporware. These fixed costs cover the outlays associated with retooling existing plant equipment and the specific research and development efforts associated with perfecting any new product formulation.

As of quarter 1, each of your two vaporware brands has the formulation 30/30/30/5/5/5/5. Some brands are actively distributed in various BRANDS™ regions as of quarter 1. An introduction of currently-inactive brands into other BRANDS™ market regions does not necessarily require a reformulation, if you are satisfied that their existing formulations are satisfactory for your purposes.

In BRANDS™, reformulations are accomplished by submitting such requests along with all other decision variable change requests. See Chapter 8 for a description of the various BRANDS™ decision variable change request forms.

Reformulations of existing vaporware brands should presumably only be undertaken after extensive product testing via the various BRANDS™ marketing research capabilities. Given that preferences may vary across the BRANDS™ market regions, it is easy to imagine that a firm might eventually develop a range of different vaporware brands, perhaps targeted to specific BRANDS™ regions. Of course, it is also possible that specific preferences for product compositions do not really vary that much from region to region, so perhaps there is one all-purpose generic vaporware brand formulation that will be well received throughout the BRANDS™ world.

Since reformulations involve considerable work for your plant management, your research and development staff, your advertising agency, and your sales force, corporate policy limits reformulations in any quarter to a maximum of one.

When a vaporware brand is reformulated, a number of things happen. First, experience has been gained by your research and development group in product quality improvements is completely lost when a reformulation occurs. Among other consequences, this may translate into some short-term problems in quality control and quality assurance. This may lead customers to have some initial doubts as to the quality of your newly reformulated brand. Second, any experience curve effects on production costs are lost upon reformulation. Experience accumulates for the new formulation from a starting point of zero. See Chapter 4 for information on experience curve effects. Third, the general level of brand loyalty and goodwill associated with brands tends to carry-over after reformulations. No doubt some customers are lost after any reformulation, but the numbers have never been thought to be particularly large. However, it must be expected that the carry-over of customer and dealer brand loyalty to the newly reformulated brand will depend on the similarity of the old brand composition to the new. Large changes in a brand's composition may lead brand-loyal customers to reconsider their brand preferences and assess whether a newly reformulated brand still meets their needs. Of course, if a reformulated brand is substantially more preferred than its old formulation, then presumably many new customers are attracted to the reformulated brand.

Reminder: Reformulations must satisfy vaporware technology constraints. Technologically-infeasible reformulation requests are not processed and the previous formulation of a vaporware brand remains in effect.

Research and Development Decisions

Firms may choose to allocate funds to their research and development groups to aid in brand quality improvements. Although there are no absolute minimums in this regard, it is generally thought that at least $10,000 per quarter should be allocated to research and development in support of each brand that a firm is actively marketing. Additional funds allow for further research and development staff to be deployed to support product quality improvement efforts.

Product quality improvements tend to require sustained effort on the part of your research and development group over an extended time frame. Thus, it should be expected that a continual flow of funds tends to work much better than occasional large expenditure levels. Experience suggests that vaporware brands are only rarely successful for long if expenditures on research and development are low.

The value of research and development efforts have never really been clearly established in the vaporware industry. There is no generally agreed upon yardstick with which to measure the effectiveness of research and development efforts. However, many industry analysts maintain that the impact of research and development expenditures and activities is ultimately felt on the quality perceptions that customers hold for vaporware brands.

There are limits on research and development spending changes from one quarter to the next for each vaporware brand. Specifically, research and development spending support may not increase by more than $250,000 for each brand from the previous quarter's research and development spending level. Thus, a larger research and development budget increase, for example, would have to be phased in over several quarters. Research and development spending may be reduced to any amount, including $0, at any time. Note that if research and development spending support is $0 in any quarter, then the maximum possible research and development spending level in the following quarter is $250,000.

Product Preference and Product Quality

In BRANDS™, a product's formulation influences the preference that customers have for it (*product preference*). Research and development spending, in the main, is ultimately translated in *product quality* perceptions. *Product preference* and *product quality* are two different and unrelated constructs in BRANDS™.

To illustrate the differences, consider the choice of a restaurant for a special dining-out occasion. Here, "product preference" would depend on such things as food selection, service, ambience, and the like. "Product quality" would refer to the actual quality of the food, given the particular food selection and specialization. In this context, a restaurant specializing in seafood might score very high on "product quality" (if it has good seafood) but very low on "product preference" for someone with an aversion to seafood. Alternatively, a fine sports car might score highly on "product preference" for someone who values such aspects of automobiles, but very low on "product quality" if it is unreliable transportation.

In summary, product preference and product quality are different things, and high performance on one does not necessarily imply corresponding excellence on the other.

New Product Development and Introduction

The introduction of a new vaporware brand in BRANDS™ should presumably be preceded by product testing research. A range of marketing research studies are available to assist you in these new product development endeavors. See Chapter 5 for details.

New products may be created within BRANDS™. Brands must be explicitly introduced into BRANDS™ regions. Actual introduction into the marketplace occurs immediately.

Note that vaporware brands may be actively distributed in one or more of the three market regions. There is no need to have complete distribution of a vaporware brand in all market regions.

It is possible to delay actual brand introduction to permit pre-launch marketing support efforts to be initiated prior to actual launch. Thus, you may decide to allocate marketing support expenditures to advertising, sales force, and research and development prior to actually launching a brand. Any such marketing support spending occurs immediately after you authorize it. Such pre-launch marketing efforts may speed the introduction process by making dealers and customers aware of the existence of the impending launch. Of course, such activities may also come to the attention of alert competitors.

Brands may be dropped from active distribution in any or all regions. Such brand deletion decisions are implemented immediately. After a brand is dropped from active distribution, it is also necessary to ensure that the advertising and promotion support spending levels are changed to zero and that any sales force time allocation for the deleted brand is reallocated to other active brands.

Dropping a brand from active distribution does not, in itself, alter the marketing support activities associated with it.

New product development activity should be viewed as an integral component of each BRANDS™ firm's marketing strategy. The actual out-of-pocket costs of introducing a new product may be only a very small component of the total new product development costs. The major costs of new product development activity are undoubtedly incurred in the marketing research efforts related to designing a product that will be well-received by customers.

To introduce a vaporware brand into any of the BRANDS™ regions costs $400,000. These are fixed setup costs incurred to convince dealers of the merits of stocking your particular brand of vaporware. The costs are charged on the introducing firm's operating statements in the quarter in which actual brand introduction occurs.

Introductions and reformulations are completely separate and independent decisions. In BRANDS™, an "introduction" refers to the decision to actively distribute a brand in a region or regions; "reformulation" refers to changing a brand's formulation. After a reformulation, a brand does not have to be re-introduced into markets in which it is already being actively distributed. However, a brand reformulated and specifically targeted for one or more regions in which it is not yet actively distributed must be formally introduced into the targeted markets.

A brand may be reformulated without being introduced and an existing brand may be introduced into one or more markets without being reformulated. In the latter case, the brand would be introduced with its current formulation. Presumably, such a decision would be based on some marketing research which indicates the potential attractiveness of the existing formulation to customers in the targeted region(s).

Distribution Considerations

Vaporware is sold widely by various dealers and sales agents (for the industrial segment) and in various dealer outlets (for the consumer segment), including general purpose types of stores (that is, department stores) and specialty stores. In the vaporware industry, such dealers, sales agents, and dealer outlets are collectively referred to as "dealers." Dealers purchase vaporware directly from the various competing firms in the vaporware industry. Exclusive dealership arrangements do not exist in the vaporware industry.

Dealers' stocking decisions (and the amount of space, resources, and effort allocated to the vaporware product category and to any particular vaporware brand) are thought to be based largely on return-on-investment kinds of criteria. That is, dealers generally desire to stock and support products that have a high markup potential, a large volume, and no need for special handling. All vaporware brands satisfy the "no special handling" criterion without any problems. High markup would be associated with the higher-priced brands (since dealers use a fairly standard cost-plus pricing strategy), while actual volume or turnover would depend on customer acceptance (that is, market share).

Sales force efforts are thought to be of value in encouraging dealers to stock and support vaporware brands. Firms may direct their sales forces to allocate their efforts among various brands. For example, it is possible to direct the sales force to emphasize support of a new product being introduced into a market region, to attempt to ensure that it receives adequate distribution coverage. When a firm has more than one brand being actively distributed in a market region, the firm may specify how the sales force is to allocate its available selling time in support of its brands. These time allocations are expressed in percentage.

Pricing Decisions

BRANDS™ firms control the list price of brands. The list price is the manufacturer's price for vaporware. List prices may vary for each vaporware brand in each of the market regions.

Vaporware is sold through dealers in each BRANDS™ market region. The average markup percentages that dealers currently employ in arriving at their respective selling prices for the vaporware product category are as follows: market region #1 ("U.S.A."), 55%; market region #2 ("Europe"), 65%; and, market region #3 ("Pacific"), 70%. As an illustrative example of these markups, an $800 manufacturer list price quoted in the Pacific market region would translate into a $1,360 dealer price.

Experience in the vaporware market has shown that demand is sensitive to price in the usual fashion: customers prefer lower priced vaporware brands, holding all other relevant factors constant. For market shares, customer choice of any particular brand of vaporware is partially based on the brand's price relative to the prices of competing brands of vaporware. Frequent price changes seem to upset dealers, sometimes causing some to discontinue selling such vaporware brands.

While there seems to be some degree of brand loyalty toward vaporware brands, price changes tend to upset such loyalty and cause formerly brand-loyal customers to look around and consider purchasing other brands. A vaporware brand price that is far below the industry norm runs the risk of having customers wonder about the quality of the low priced brand. Given natural aversion to risk on the part of customers, such concerns might lead to reductions in purchases of such a super low priced vaporware brand. Particularly high priced vaporware, even for highly desirable product formulations and even for brands that are supported with massive marketing effort (advertising, promotion, and sales force activities), are not likely to be well received by customers.

The obvious impact of price on final customers is noted above. There is another, perhaps equally important, indirect effect of pricing decisions in the vaporware industry. Dealers' margins are influenced directly by firms' prices. Since vaporware dealers follow cost-plus markup pricing rules, higher costs (manufacturers' prices) translate into more financial return (margin) per unit of vaporware sold. Of course, dealers' total profitability depends on unit margins times volume. Thus, high prices affect dealers positively and final customers negatively.

There are limits on how much a vaporware brand price may change from one quarter to the next. Specifically, prices may not increase by more than $1,000 from the previous quarter's prices. Prices may be reduced by any amount at any time, as long as a manufacturer list price of at least $100 is charged. Thus, a larger price increase, for example, would have to be phased in over several quarters. Note that a brand not actively distributed (marketed) in a quarter may have any price in the $100-$9,999 range in the following quarter.

Prices are expressed in even-dollar amounts only in BRANDS™; cents are not used.

Inactive brands' prices are irrelevant in BRANDS™. There is no need to have a price of $0 for an inactive brands. An active brand being dropped from a market may have its price left at the former value. Since an inactive brand has no sales (because it is not being actively distributed), its price is irrelevant.

Reminder: Firms do not necessarily have to charge the same price in each BRANDS™ market region in which a brand is distributed.

Advertising Decisions

Firms make decisions on the amount of money to be allocated to customer advertising in support of each vaporware brand in each BRANDS™ market region. Associated with this advertising expenditure decision are media content decisions.

In BRANDS™, media content means copy emphasis, such as an emphasis on price or product availability or guarantees. Media content may vary from region to region and from brand to brand. For example, it would be possible to use one content in support of one brand and another content in support of a second brand, even if both brands were being marketed in the same BRANDS™ market region. Also, the same brand may have different media contents across the various BRANDS™ market regions in which it is distributed.

In making advertising decisions, BRANDS™ firms are really just providing direction to their advertising agencies. The advertising agencies create copy and place it in designated media. When you change the media content associated with the advertising of one of your vaporware brands in some BRANDS™ market regions, your advertising agency has to channel some of the advertising expenditures toward the actual creation of the new copy. Thus, a reduced amount of the overall advertising budget is available for actual placement in any quarter in which a media copy change is implemented. Media content changes should probably not be made in every quarter.

There are six basic media contents available in BRANDS™: price, quality, uses, benefits, availability (frequency with which dealers stock products), and performance guarantees.

Any pairwise combination of two of these six basic media contents may be used, generating an additional fifteen possible media contents. Thus, there are a total of 21 (6+15) possible different media contents or combinations of contents that firms may choose in BRANDS™. These media contents may be thought of as different kinds of advertising copy emphases. The complete set of 21 different media contents is enumerated in Table 3.

Within BRANDS™, the effectiveness of media contents tends to vary from one market region to another. The effectiveness of media content naturally depends partially upon the brand with which it is associated. For example, even though a price message might have some level of general effectiveness, if a price message is tied to a brand whose price is among the highest in a market, it is reasonable to expect that the specific effectiveness of such a message would be substantially reduced (in comparison with the general level of effectiveness of price messages in the BRANDS™ region). The impact of advertising on customers is thought to have fairly substantial carry-over effects beyond the original quarter of the expenditure.

There are limits on how much advertising may change from one quarter to the next. Specifically, advertising spending support for any vaporware brand in any BRANDS™ market region may not increase by more than $3,000,000 from the previous quarter's advertising spending level. A larger advertising budget increase would have to be phased in over several quarters. Advertising spending may be reduced

Table 3

BRANDS™ MEDIA CONTENTS

Media Content Code	Media Content
1	Price
2	Product Quality
3	Product Uses
4	Product Benefits
5	Product Availability
6	Product Performance Guarantees
7	Price and Product Quality
8	Price and Product Uses
9	Price and Product Benefits
10	Price and Product Availability
11	Price and Product Performance Guarantees
12	Product Quality and Product Uses
13	Product Quality and Product Benefits
14	Product Quality and Product Availability
15	Product Quality and Product Performance Guarantees
16	Product Uses and Product Benefits
17	Product Uses and Product Availability
18	Product Uses and Product Performance Guarantees
19	Product Benefits and Product Availability
20	Product Benefits and Product Performance Guarantees
21	Product Availability and Product Performance Guarantees

to any amount, including $0, at any time. If advertising spending support is $0 in any quarter, then the maximum possible advertising spending level in the following quarter is $3,000,000.

Promotion Decisions

Firms may choose to allocate funds to sales promotion activities to support any brand in any market region. Promotional activities are managed by firms' regional sales managers in the various BRANDS™ market regions.

Since any promotional effort costs at least $25,000 to design and implement in a region, the first $25,000 of promotional budgets in any quarter goes toward fixed setup costs. Dollar amounts over this minimum are then available for use in executing promotional activities. Examples of promotional activities routinely conducted in the vaporware industry include special dealer volume discounts, customer rebates, special display activities at dealers' premises, special educational and training programs for dealers' sales representatives, trade show presentations and participation, special trade-in and exchange conditions, and the like. Of course, promotional activities directed at dealers presumably also influence customers, although indirectly. Also, some promotional activities involve a firm's sales force. These take the form of special sales contests and similar short-term incentive programs.

Industry experts believe that promotional activities have some impact on dealers and customers. However, the effects of such sales promotion efforts seem to be felt only in the quarter in which they are used, with little residual carry-over into subsequent quarters. In the past, promotional efforts have been used to give a brand a shot-in-the-arm, particularly in the case of new product introductions into BRANDS™ regions. They have also been used as a competitive countermeasure against new product introductions, although a still-pending anti-trust suit regarding the unnatural and predatory use of such promotional expenditures has dampened the enthusiasm of some industry participants for using promotions in such a way.

There is considerable continuing debate in the vaporware industry about how promotional budget dollars should be used. Some believe that firms should be promoting aggressively at all times. Others believe that firms should only use promotion selectively, and then with a major effort. The majority of industry experts, however, believe, that promotions of various kinds are likely to have positive effects on dealers and customers. Nevertheless, the actual profitability of promotional efforts is unknown.

There are limits on how much promotion may change from one quarter to the next. Specifically, promotion spending support for any vaporware brand in any market region may not increase by more than $5,000,000 from the previous quarter's promotion spending level. A larger promotion budget increase would have to be phased in over several quarters. Promotion spending on a vaporware brand in any market region may be reduced to any amount, including $0, at any time. Note that if promotion spending support for a brand in any market region is $0 in any quarter, then the maximum possible promotion spending level for the brand in that market region in the following quarter is $5,000,000.

Sales Force Decisions

Your division maintains a separate sales force in each market region. Sales force activities do not influence customers directly. Rather, they influence the behavior of dealers. Most reputable vaporware industry experts believe that sales force efforts can have a substantial influence on channel members' behavior.

BRANDS™ firms make three specific sales force management decisions in each region in which vaporware brands are being actively distributed: sales force compensation levels (salary and commission), sales force size, and sales force time allocation among the firm's brands. By making these various sales force management decisions, a firm is establishing policies that are executed by the regional sales manager in each BRANDS™ region. Thus, the sales force size is really an allocated level of sales representatives, and the regional sales manager establishes hiring policies to maintain that level.

BRANDS™ firms may have different sales force compensation levels (salary and commission) in the three market regions, if they choose. It has been observed that sales force motivation (and, therefore, effort and effectiveness) seems to be positively affected by salary levels. High-paying firms tend to attract more able sales representatives, who tend to be more effective in performing the sales task.

Since sales representatives tend to be quite sensitive about changes in the sales force compensation arrangements, firms should be somewhat careful about changing compensation levels too frequently. The vaporware industry norm in this regard seems to involve salary adjustments about once or, at most, twice a year.

A problem has recently arisen within the vaporware industry regarding sales force compensation. In particular, some firms have established salary policies that involve widely differing compensation levels for their various sales forces across the regions in which they are actively marketing vaporware. While cost-of-living considerations and competitive market forces might well lead a firm to have a sales force compensation policy with some variation from one region to another, levels which are substantially different from region to region are likely to lead to morale problems across all of a firm's regional sales forces, not just in the regions where compensation levels are particularly low. Such morale problems, were they actually to exist, would likely translate into lower performance, higher turnover, and other manifestations that would impede the selling effort. Thus, extreme compensation ranges may run the risk of being harmful to the performance level of a firm's sales force. Deviations in a firm's compensation levels across the BRANDS™ market regions of 10%-20% are not thought to be extreme. However, deviations of more than 50% would probably be viewed as quite extreme.

Attempts to lower sales force compensation levels (especially salaries) are viewed with substantial disfavor by sales representatives, as might be expected. Recognizing this, your firm has a general policy of not lowering sales force salaries. If a team really wants to lower sales force salaries in any market region, they will generally have to leave the salaries at a constant level and let inflation lower them (perhaps slowly!) in real terms through time. If a team feels that it is critical to make a substantial decrease in sales force salaries immediately, they have to obtain special approval from the course instructor.

Within BRANDS™, salaries are expressed in terms of dollars per month. Thus, a $24,000 per year salary would be specified as a $2,000 salary per month within BRANDS™. Commissions are based on sales revenues. Sales commissions are limited to the range 1%-9% in integer amounts. Sales Overhead is based on total sales force compensation (salaries plus commissions).

Firms are free to vary the size of their sales force complements in each BRANDS™ market region. However, there are certain costs associated with hiring new sales representatives and in firing existing sales representatives. The cost of hiring a new sales representative is equal to one month's salary. This represents the costs associated with recruiting, screening, and hiring. Reducing the current sales force in a BRANDS™ market region requires a lump-sum settlement equal to two months' salary. It has been observed in the past that newly hired sales representatives tend not to be as effective as existing sales representatives for the first quarter or so. Part of this reduced effectiveness is attributable to your firm's standard sales training program which each new representative completes.

Transferring sales representatives from one region to another is equivalent to firing the representatives in the originating region and then hiring them in the destination region. Thus, there are no cost savings associated with transferring sales representatives.

Firms may direct their sales managers in each market region to allocate the efforts of their available sales representatives to support each vaporware brand in active distribution. These time allocations are expressed in percentage terms. Firms with only a single brand in a region have 100% of their sales force's time allocated to that brand. With two brands in a region, any combination of time allocation percentages (such as 50% and 50%, or 10% and 90%) is possible so long as they sum to 100% across the vaporware brands. Experience suggests that efforts at pushing products through the channel of distribution have had some success.

Within BRANDS™, teams control sales force size (the number of sales representatives) and sales force time allocations across brands. BRANDS™ calculates sales force effort as being equal to the product of sales force size and time allocation percentage. For example, a sales force size of 200 representatives in a market region and a 50% time allocation to a particular brand in the region would result in a sales force effort of $(200)(0.50) = 100$, which is interpreted as the equivalent of 100 sales representatives being used to support the brand in the market region.

Each sales representative incurs standard expenses in connection with the sales task. These expenses involve both direct and indirect components. Direct expenses generated are in terms of fringe benefits (health insurance, government taxes of various kinds, and so on) and travel costs (automobile costs and per diem expenses while away from home). Indirect costs to support the sales representative include periodic sales training activities, sales management overhead, office support, and the like. In total, these expenses are equal to the compensation (salary and commission) level of a sales representative. Thus, if you have a monthly sales force salary level of $2,500 and 0% commission in a BRANDS™ market region, a further $2,500 of sales force expenses per month are also incurred to support the sales representative. Your division is billed automatically for the direct and indirect costs associated with maintaining sales representatives in each of the market regions in which you choose to have an active sales force. These sales expenses are recorded as Sales Overhead.

While it is not required that you maintain a sales force in each of the BRANDS™ market regions, you may not do very well in securing and maintaining distribution coverage for your brands if they are not supported by appropriate sales force efforts.

There are limits on how much sales force size and sales force salary may change from quarter to the next. Specifically, sales force size may not increase by more than fifty from the previous quarter's sales force size level; any level of sales force size reduction may be effected at any time. In particular, sales force size may be reduced to zero at any time. Sales force salary may not change by more than $500 from the previous quarter's sales force salary level. (Sales force salaries may not decrease, without special permission from the course instructor.) Larger sales force size or sales force salary increases would have to be phased in over several quarters. Note that if sales force size is zero in any quarter, then the maximum possible sales force size in the following quarter is fifty.

Sales Forecasting Decisions

Although not usually categorized as a marketing mix decision variable, sales forecasting decisions are inevitably required of all practicing marketing managers. Good sales forecasting requires a careful balancing between inventory levels and stock-outs, both of which are costly. Sales forecasting prowess also represents an important signal as to a BRANDS™ team's basic understanding of the marketplace in which it competes.

Sales volume forecasts for every active brand in every region are required in each quarter. As with all BRANDS™ decision variables, sales forecasts are considered permanent, until they are changed. If you are satisfied with the previous quarter's sales forecast value, then no action is required. However, since sales volumes are influenced by both your marketing program and by those of your rivals, sales forecasts are likely to be the most frequently-changed BRANDS™ decision variable. This probably means sales volume forecasts will need to be updated every quarter for every brand in every region.

Sales forecasting accuracy is one of the mechanisms by which a team's performance may be evaluated. Sales forecasting accuracy is one of the components of Operating Efficiency, described in Chapter 7. Also, a separate Sales Forecasting Accuracy Score exists in BRANDS™. It is reported when Marketing Research Study #16 is requested.

Within BRANDS™, sales forecasts are evaluated on the basis of how close they are to the actual sales volume realization in each quarter. The evaluation mechanism is as follows: a sales volume forecast within 1% of actual sales volume receives 100 points; a sales volume forecast within 2% of actual sales volume receives 99 points; and so on down to a sales volume forecast within 99% of actual sales volume which yields 1 point. Sales forecasts which vary by more than 100% above or below actual sales volumes receive no points. The evaluation for each team is then based on the average sales forecasting points achieved per forecast.

Sales volume forecasting accuracy influences the overhead costs associated with each product in each market region in which it is active (Administrative Overhead). This situation reflects the implicit and explicit costs associated with poor sales forecasts. Sales volume forecasts represent important inputs into manpower planning, facilities planning, production scheduling, and cash management processes. Errors in such forecasts have costly consequences.

Regional fixed costs equal the base fixed costs only if the corresponding sales volume forecast has an accuracy score of 100. With a sales volume forecasting accuracy score of 0, fixed costs double the base costs. Values of sales forecasting accuracy between 100 and 0 linearly increase fixed costs from their base value to twice their base value. For example, a sales volume forecasting accuracy score of 78 results in fixed costs being equal to 1.22 times the base costs.

Sales forecasts are only "scored" (that is, counted in the Sales Forecasting Accuracy Score) when the associated vaporware brand market share in a quarter is at least 2.5% in a BRANDS™ region. This is meant to alleviate the sales forecasting problems associated with new product launches, which may be very unpredictable.

Two marketing research studies (Marketing Research Study #31 and #32) provide some assistance to those making sales volume forecasting decisions. However, potential users of these marketing research studies are cautioned that these sales volume forecasts are simply extrapolative in nature. They assume that the direction and pattern of current marketing efforts of all firms, both your firm and all competitors, remain the same in the next quarter. For more details about these marketing research studies, see Chapter 5.

BRANDS™ Marketing Decision Variable Change Limits

As described earlier in this chapter, BRANDS™ marketing decision variables have built-in limitations related to how much they may change from one quarter to the next. For reference purposes, these limitations are summarized in Table 4.

Table 4

MAXIMUM POSSIBLE CHANGES IN BRANDS™ MARKETING
DECISION VARIABLES

Decision Variable	Maximum Permissible Increase From One Quarter To The Next
Advertising	$3,000,000 per brand per region, but advertising may be reduced to any amount below its current level (including $0) at any time.
Price	$1,000 per brand per region, but price may be reduced to any amount below its current level at any time, as long as the price is not less than $100. (Note: A brand not actively distributed in a BRANDS™ market region in a quarter may have any price in the $100-$9,999 range in the following quarter.)
Promotion	$5,000,000 per brand per region, but promotion may be reduced to any amount below its current level (including $0) at any time.
Research and Development	$250,000 per brand, but research and development may be reduced to any amount (including $0) at any time.
Sales Force Salary	$500 per region. (Note: Sales force salary decreases are not possible, without special permission from the course instructor.)
Sales Force Size	50 per region, but sales force size may be reduced to any level (including zero) at any time.

Chapter 4

Non-Marketing Decision Variables

Introduction

Non-marketing decision variables and cost-related parameters are described in this chapter of the BRANDS™ participant's manual.

Operations Management

In BRANDS™, production and plant capacity management occurs automatically. By shifting production capacity among its various product lines (one of which is vaporware), your plant is always at "full capacity" — that is, your vaporware plant capacity is always equal to current sales volume. Also, since just enough production is ordered automatically to meet current sales volume, no finished goods inventory exists in BRANDS™.

Plant capacity depreciates each quarter, one part of the depreciation being related to actual plant usage (variable depreciation) and another part being independent of usage (fixed depreciation). In each quarter, fixed depreciation charges are equal to 3% of the current plant capacity value. In addition, another 12% of current plant capacity depreciates in the form of variable depreciation.

Product-Related Costs

Your plant charges your vaporware operating division for the costs associated with manufacturing vaporware. The cost of goods sold (per unit) may be expressed, approximately, in the following terms:

$$COGS = RMCOST + LCOST + PRCOST + PDCOST + PKCOST$$

where: COGS is total cost of goods sold ($ per unit) at the plant, not including cost-adjustment premiums for vaporware brands with Compatibility and Warranty levels above the minimum level; RMCOST is raw materials cost ($ per unit); LCOST is labor cost ($ per unit); PRCOST is production processing costs (in $ per unit); PDCOST is variable cost ($ per unit) of plant depreciation attributable to a specific vaporware brand; and, PKCOST is packaging cost ($ per unit). The cost-adjustment premiums associated with vaporware brands with non-minimum Compatibility and Warranty levels are described below.

PDCOST is based on plant capacity utilization. It reflects the variable depreciation of plant capacity associated with vaporware production. Variable depreciation cost is currently 12%. With a $400 per unit capacity charge, this amounts to $48 per unit in variable depreciation charges.

The current costs of the other components of COGS are as follows: LCOST is $15.00 per unit, PRCOST is $30.00 per unit, and PKCOST is $10.00 per unit. These costs are generally negotiated with your plant on a yearly basis. Since your plant operates as a separate profit center, it negotiates fixed cost contracts with your plant. These costs will be in effect until the end of the next game year. In the recent past, these costs have increased roughly with the inflation rate.

The current raw materials cost per pound for each of the five basic raw materials in vaporware are as follows: Syntech, $25.00; Plumbo, $35.00; Glomp, $15.00; Trimicro, $10.00; and, Fralange, $5.00. Your plant negotiates yearly contracts with several suppliers of these raw materials, so these raw materials costs normally do not change throughout a BRANDS™ year.

The purchasing agent at your plant has well-established working relationships with all major suppliers. Since the raw materials ingredients are essentially commodities with only a single grade being available, raw materials prices posted by suppliers tend to be virtually identical to each other. Your purchasing agent typically splits purchases about equally among the major raw materials suppliers, so as not to be overly dependent on any single supplier.

Raw materials prices have generally increased about equally with changes in the consumer price index. However, this is not true for Plumbo, which is a petroleum derivative. Plumbo's costs have increased as much as 25% in some recent years, although with the current world oil situation some stability in the price of Plumbo is anticipated.

Given the above information, the total raw materials costs, RMCOST, associated with each unit of vaporware can be expressed in the following terms:

$$RMCOST = 3*(25.00*WS + 35.00*WP + 15.00*WG + 10.00*WT + 5.00*WF)$$

where WS, WP, WG, WT, and WF are the proportions of the vaporware brand compositions of Syntech, Plumbo, Glomp, Trimicro, and Fralange, respectively.

The cost-of-goods-sold figure described earlier is based on vaporware with Compatibility and Warranty both equal to 1. Compatibility and Warranty levels above 1 affect total costs as follows. Each increment above the values of 1 for Compatibility and Warranty adds a premium of 1.0% and 1.2% of costs, respectively, times the square of the amount of the product attribute value above 1 to the overall costs associated with a vaporware brand. These costs are compounded (that is, multiplied).

To illustrate the variable cost impact of the sixth and seventh vaporware product attributes, consider first a 10/30/50/ 5/ 5/1/1 vaporware brand. Such a brand of vaporware would cost $63.75 per unit in raw materials. This total cost per unit is derived as follows:

$$3[\$25.00(0.10) + \$35.00(0.30) + \$15.00(0.50) + \$10.00(0.05) + \$5.00(0.05)] = \$63.75.$$

In addition, other manufacturing costs (production, labor, packaging, and variable depreciation) would amount to an additional $30+$15+$10+$48 = $103, assuming that the firm is operating at full capacity and that no production smoothing cost adjustments are necessary. Thus, excluding Compatibility and Warranty adjustments, the total per unit manufacturing costs for a 10/30/50/ 5/ 5/1/1 vaporware brand would amount to $166.75. Note that there are no extra cost impacts of Compatibility and Warranty levels in this case, since they are both equal to their minimum value, 1.

Alternatively, the vaporware brand 10/30/50/ 5/ 5/5/6 would also cost $166.75 in terms of basic manufacturing costs, but the impacts of the Compatibility of 5 and the Warranty of 6 are substantial. The total per unit cost, including the Compatibility and Warranty cost-adjustment premiums, would be: $166.75*[1+0.010(5-1)(5-1)]*[1+0.012(6-1)(6-1)]= (166.75)*(1.16)*(1.30) = \$251.46$. As may be noted, high levels of Compatibility and Warranty have a substantial influence on costs. The maximum levels of Compatibility and Warranty, 9 in each case, would have a cost impact of

$$[1+0.010(9-1)(9-1)][1+0.012(9-1)(9-1)] = [1.64][1.77] = 2.90$$

on a vaporware brand. This represents a 190% cost premium impact, above and beyond all other manufacturing costs, to achieve the maximum levels of Compatibility and Warranty.

Cost-adjustment premiums associated with all possible combinations of Compatibility and Warranty are shown in Table 5.

Table 5

COST PREMIUMS FOR VARIOUS COMPATIBILITY AND WARRANTY LEVELS

		Compatibility								
		1	2	3	4	5	6	7	8	9
Warranty	1	1.000	1.010	1.040	1.090	1.160	1.250	1.360	1.490	1.650
	2	1.012	1.022	1.052	1.103	1.174	1.265	1.376	1.508	1.660
	3	1.048	1.058	1.090	1.142	1.216	1.310	1.425	1.562	1.719
	4	1.108	1.119	1.152	1.208	1.285	1.385	1.507	1.651	1.817
	5	1.192	1.204	1.240	1.299	1.383	1.490	1.621	1.776	1.955
	6	1.300	1.313	1.352	1.417	1.508	1.625	1.768	1.937	2.132
	7	1.432	1.446	1.489	1.561	1.661	1.790	1.948	2.134	2.348
	8	1.588	1.604	1.652	1.731	1.842	1.985	2.160	2.366	2.604
	9	1.768	1.786	1.839	1.927	2.051	2.210	2.404	2.634	2.900

Notes:
(1) These cost-adjustment premiums are applied to the total cost of a vaporware brand, including raw materials, production, labor, packaging, and variable depreciation costs.
(2) Example: A vaporware brand with a total cost of $150 per unit, and Compatibility and Warranty levels of 3 and 7, respectively, would have overall cost of $150*1.489 = \$223.35$, after including the cost premiums adjustments associated with Compatibility and Warranty.

Experience Curve Effects and Product Costs

Based on recent technological advancements in the manufacture of vaporware, your plant now believes that it is possible to realize experience curve effects. These experience curve effects lower the variable costs associated with vaporware manufacturing. Experience curve effects operate at the level of an individual brand and result in reduced unit costs associated with production and labor costs and, separately, for raw materials — but not for variable plant depreciation and not for packaging costs.

Experience (cumulative production volume) accumulates only for a specific brand formulation. A reformulation of a brand's composition results in all production experience on that brand being lost. The Production Cost Analysis Report in the regular financial and operating statements may be consulted for some information on current costs and levels of cumulative production experience.

Experience curve effects are felt only after some minimum cumulative production experience (volume) has been achieved with a specific brand formulation. Experience curve adjustments on base costs occur only for the cumulative production experience in excess of this minimum. The precise values of the minimum level and the shape of the cost savings with cumulative experience are not known with certainty at this time. Only experience will reveal their possible magnitudes.

Cumulative production experience curve effects only accrue to an existing formulation of a brand. All experience-based cost savings are lost upon a reformulation. Thus, cost savings accrue to brands whose formulations remain constant through time.

Since raw material, production, and labor costs account for the majority of vaporware product costs, experience curve effects have the potential — if large enough — to materially reduce variable product costs.

Transportation and Shipping Costs

By arrangement with the various dealers in all BRANDS™ market regions, your firm pays for the transportation and shipping costs associated with having vaporware orders delivered to the dealers. For the domestic market, shipping is via truck transportation from your plant. Overseas markets involve trucking  to a suitable domestic seaport, container vessel transportation to an appropriate seaport in Europe or the Pacific market region, and local truck transportation.

The current total transportation and shipping costs to each of the market regions are as follows: Region #1 (U.S.A.), $25.00 per unit; Region #2 (Europe), $50.00 per unit; and, Region #3 (Pacific), $75.00 per unit. These transportation and shipping charges are for each unit of vaporware, regardless of formulation.

In the past, transportation and shipping costs have increased through time approximately at the rate of inflation.

General Overhead Charges

Corporate overhead is charged on a per-active-brand-per-quarter basis. This charge appears as Corporate Overhead on the Divisional Operating Statement. The current Corporate Overhead charge is $500,000 per active brand per quarter. In addition, Administrative Overhead of $500,000 per quarter is charged to your division for each BRANDS™ region in which each brand is in active distribution. This $500,000 Administrative Overhead base amount is predicated on a sales volume forecasting accuracy of 100. As described in Chapter 3, sales volume forecast inaccuracies can double this base Administrative Overhead value.

Note that this adjustment in Administrative Overhead cost is made for all active brands, even for those with market shares of less than 2.5% in a BRANDS™ market region. Although sales forecast accuracy scores are not counted for small market share brands (that is, those with a market share in a BRANDS™ market region of less than 2.5%), sales forecasting accuracy does affect the Administrative Overhead cost for all brands, regardless of their market shares.

Taxation

The corporate tax rate in the vaporware industry is currently 50%. This tax rate is levied on the total income (operating and non-operating income) of your division.

If your division has negative income in any quarter, the application of this tax results in negative tax being due. Such negative tax is a tax credit that is used to offset future tax obligations. All payments of taxes and applications of tax credits to future tax obligations are handled automatically by the BRANDS™ software.

Banking Arrangements

Provisions exist in BRANDS™ for automatic lines of credit (bank loans) to be extended and for investments of excess cash in short-term marketable securities to occur as the occasion arises.

When the game first runs, any existing bank loans are paid off and any existing marketable securities are sold off. After the game runs, cash on hand is examined. If cash on hand is less than 8% of the quarter's sales revenues, an immediate loan is taken out to raise current cash on hand to this level. If cash is more than 12% of the quarter's sales revenues, then the excess is immediately invested in short-term (one quarter) marketable securities. Thus, a firm never has both a loan and a short-term investment in marketable securities simultaneously. These operations are performed automatically within BRANDS™.

The normal cost of short-term loans is currently 3% per quarter, which is the current prime rate of interest in BRANDS™. This 3% interest rate is applicable if outstanding loans do not exceed 20% of net assets. Net assets are equal to total assets less outstanding loans, if any. (Net assets are also equal to common stock plus retained earnings.)

For firms whose outstanding bank loans in any quarter exceed 20% of net assets, higher interest rate charges are payable. These interest premiums reflect the risk situation associated with relatively highly levered firms. The complete current interest rate schedule for outstanding loans in the vaporware industry is as follows:

Interest Rate	Relationship Between Loans and Net Assets
3%	If Loans/Net Assets ≤ 0.20
4%	If 0.20 < Loans/Net Assets ≤ 0.30
5%	If 0.30 < Loans/Net Assets ≤ 0.40
6%	If 0.40 < Loans/Net Assets ≤ 0.50
9%	If Loans/Net Assets > 0.50

This interest-rate schedule is based on a normal interest rate of 3%. If the prime rate applicable to the vaporware industry changes, all of the other interest rates in this schedule would be subject to possible revision.

Short-term investments in marketable securities currently yield 1.75% interest per quarter.

The interest payments on bank loans and the interest received from investments in marketable securities are reported as Non-Operating Income on the firm's Divisional Operating Statement each quarter. Bank loan interest charges would represent negative Non-Operating Income.

On the Divisional Operating Statement, Non-Operating Income is based on the marketable securities or loan position at the end of the previous quarter. Thus, if loans are present at the end of quarter "n", then the Non-Operating Income in quarter "n+1" is negative (corresponding to interest paid on the loans).

Refinancing Arrangements and Dividends

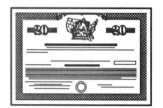

Each quarter in which your net income is positive, BRANDS™ automatically issues a dividend equal to one-third of your net income on that quarter. Dividends are not issued in quarters in which your firm loses money. Dividends reduce cash, on the asset side of the balance sheet, and liabilities and equities (capitalization), on the liabilities and equities side of the balance sheet. Since dividends reduce a firm's cash, they correspondingly reduce a firm's capitalization. It follows that a dividend reduces the "I" (Investment) in "ROI" (Return-on-Investment).

Cash Flow in BRANDS™

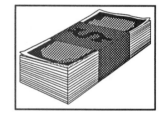

Just as in all businesses, management of cash flow is important in BRANDS™. BRANDS™ firms can never run out of cash, due to the provision for automatic loans. However, high levels of loans compared to a firm's capital base (common stock and retained earnings) result in substantial interest rate penalties on loans.

The marketable securities and loans positions can vary from quarter to quarter due to balance sheet activities (inventory and plant capacity) as well as due to operations activities (profit and loss). Sources of cash in BRANDS™ include: profits derived from operations; reduction in finished goods inventory levels; and, reductions in plant capacity levels through depreciation. Uses of cash in BRANDS™ include: losses from operations (especially related to new product launches); investments in finished goods inventories; new investment in plant capacity; and, payment of dividends.

The BRANDS™ Stock Market

BRANDS™ has its own stock market in which all vaporware industry firms' stock prices are reported. Stock prices are thought to reflect future earnings potential as well as recent past performance. Current stock prices (at the end of each quarter) are reported along with firms' other financial and operating results. Stock prices for all firms are $100 at the end of the initial BRANDS™ quarter, quarter 1.

What determines stock prices in BRANDS™? Presumably, the same things that influence stock prices on all stock exchanges. In the most general terms, financial theory and empirical results suggest that investors' future earnings expectations are the key drivers of current stock prices. What influences investors' future earnings expectations? Factors such as the current levels and trends in sales volume, market share, revenues, margins, profits, and operating efficiency are likely key influencers of investors' future earnings expectations. Absolute and relative (compared to other vaporware firms) considerations presumably both matter. New product launch activity normally receives special scrutiny in financial markets. Current earnings, of course, are presumably the primary factor influencing current stock prices.

Information Systems Costs

Firms are charged for information systems usage. For billing purposes, this charge is recorded as Marketing Research Study #55. The current charge is $1,000 per page of BRANDS™ output (financial and operating statement results plus marketing research results). These costs are recorded in the quarter after they are incurred, like other marketing research charges.

Naming Your Firm

Firms are referenced within BRANDS™ by their firm number. However, you may select a firm name and it will be displayed at the top of each page of your financial reports and marketing research results. Choose your firm name and advise your course instructor. Your course instructor must arrange to have the name entered into the BRANDS™ data base; you cannot do this yourself. BRANDS™ firm names may be a maximum of 50 standard typewriter-keyboard characters in length. You may change your firm name at any time.

Chapter 5

BRANDS™ Marketing Research Studies

Introduction

The marketing research studies currently available for purchase in BRANDS™ are described in this chapter of the BRANDS™ participant's manual.

Marketing research studies are primarily provided by your marketing research supplier, although some marketing research information is provided by the Vaporware Industry Trade Association. The vaporware industry marketing research supplier is well thought of in the marketing research supplier community, so you should have reasonable confidence in the general accuracy of the marketing research supplied. Of course, specific marketing research study types have strengths and weaknesses just as they do in the real world.

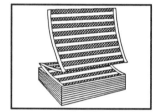

To execute a marketing research study, you complete the BRANDS™ marketing research study pre-order request form. This form may be found in Chapter 8. This form must be submitted along with any other forms (required to effect changes in marketing and non-marketing decisions, described in Chapters 3 and 4) by the specified time deadlines for each game run. A catalog of available BRANDS™ marketing research studies may be found in Table 6.

Although marketing research is requested prior to a quarter, marketing research studies are executed after a quarter has concluded. Thus, marketing research reports always reflect the just-completed quarter's experience.

Marketing Research Strategy in BRANDS™

BRANDS™ is a competitive marketing strategy game. As such, participants focus continuously on issues associated with marketing analysis, strategy, and planning. However, the details associated with implementing and executing marketing strategies and plans are not a part of BRANDS™. It follows that BRANDS™ participants do not design/place specific advertising copy in media outlets, recruit/train/supervise sales representatives, order raw materials and schedule production runs, or conduct marketing research. These things are all implicitly taken care of by your firm's advertising agency, sales managers, plant

Table 6

A CATALOG OF BRANDS™ MARKETING RESEARCH STUDIES

Product Development and Testing Research	2	Brand Composition Analysis
	12	Concept Testing
	13	Preference Testing, Two Existing Brands
	14	Preference Testing, One Existing and One Hypothetical Brand
	47	Self-Reported Attribute Preferences
Competitive and Market Monitoring Research	1	Competitive Information — Dividends and Earnings
	5	Industry Sales Force Compensation
	8	Media Content Analysis
	11	Customer Brand Awareness
	16	Operating Statistics Report
	17	Brand Quality Ratings
	21	Brand Perceptual Ratings
	27	Dealer Promotion Awareness
	28	Dealer Availability
	41	Regional Summary Analysis
Marketing Program Analysis and Evaluation	20	Test Marketing Experiment
	29	Competitive Position Audit
	35	Advertising Program Experiment
Sales Forecasting	31	Industry Sales Volume Forecasts
	32	Brand Sales Volume Forecasts

management staff, and marketing research suppliers, respectively. In essence, BRANDS™ participants receive information from various sources (internal company information systems and marketing research suppliers, in particular) and, based on that information, make decisions and communicate these decisions via decision forms or by direct data entry with BRANDS™ program B_INPUT. Others actually implement and execute your decisions.

The military metaphor immediately comes to mind to describe your situation in BRANDS™. Your team members are the officers (managers) commanding your forces (products, plant capacity, financial resources, and marketing program elements). You are located at headquarters, which is some distance from the actual battle field (the marketplace). Based on regular reports from the field (financial and operating reports) and special reconnaissance that you request (marketing research), you analyze the situation, choose strategies (select marketing program elements), make decisions, and communicate those decisions to your field officers. The field officers actually implement your decisions. Just as you do not have to be on the actual battle field to direct a successful military campaign, you do not have to be in the actual marketplace to design a successful marketing program. However, you cannot be successful in either the military battle field or the commercial marketplace without information.

Given that you cannot actually talk to other employees, your sales force, dealers, or customers, the role and importance of marketing research becomes readily apparent. Furthermore, since vaporware is an unspecified generic product, you cannot necessarily use standard rules-of-thumb (for example, "price high since vaporware customers are price insensitive") to assist you in BRANDS™. You will have to use the routinely-provided financial and operating reports plus marketing research studies that you specifically request to provide the information necessary to manage your BRANDS™ firm's affairs.

Many marketing research studies are available in BRANDS™. The existence of these marketing research studies is based on several premises:

- Marketing research is a routine fact of life in marketing. Since BRANDS™ attempts to simulate marketing management to the fullest possible extent, it is only natural that marketing research opportunities would both exist and be a normal component of the marketing management activities within BRANDS™.

- Marketing research is not free. Quite the contrary is true. Marketing research can be extraordinarily expensive in BRANDS™, if not well-managed. BRANDS™ marketing research studies have prices that are meant to be approximately representative of what such studies cost in the real world. The marketing research studies in BRANDS™ range in price from a few hundred dollars to a few hundred thousand dollars. Be thoughtful! It is possible to spend many hundreds of thousands of dollars on marketing research in a single quarter. Such spending has important consequences for current profitability. (Of course, some might argue that such spending on marketing research now is the only way to ensure future profitability.)

- The existence of a particular marketing research study in BRANDS™ is not an implicit endorsement that such a marketing research study is important, relevant, or even useful in the context of managing vaporware brands. Rather, these marketing research studies are included in BRANDS™ because they exist in the real world and real-world managers sometimes or frequently use such studies. You will have to form your own opinions about whether these studies are valuable and worth their costs in the context of BRANDS™ and the vaporware industry.

- There is normally a lag between ordering marketing research and receiving the associated study results. In BRANDS™, this is simulated by the need to pre-order marketing research studies along with all other BRANDS™ decisions.

- The sophisticated nature of the BRANDS™ exercise implies the need for sophisticated marketing research capabilities. Indeed, BRANDS™ has, by a considerable measure, the most extensive and sophisticated battery of marketing research studies of any commercially-available marketing simulation game.

All marketing research studies in BRANDS™ are quantitative in nature. Qualitative research capabilities (such as focus groups and other exploratory research procedures) are not available. Furthermore, all marketing research results are in raw form. Only the direct results of the marketing research effort are reported in BRANDS™. No managerial interpretation is provided. You must interpret the results of these marketing research studies yourself. Your interpretation efforts may require additional analysis, comparisons with previous results (from marketing research studies received in earlier quarters), and the like.

In thinking about marketing research strategy and tactics in BRANDS™, some broad generalizations seem possible:

- Excellent marketing strategy can only be developed based on excellent marketing analysis and thinking. Since marketing research provides the raw data to perform excellent marketing analysis, marketing research should be an important component of your BRANDS™ decision making process. Do not relegate your marketing research pre-ordering decisions to the last five minutes of team meetings. Rather, treat marketing research ordering decisions as a fundamental part of your whole BRANDS™ decision making process.

- Plan ahead. To identify market patterns and trends, you will probably need to order some marketing research studies on a more-or-less regular basis. A formal marketing research plan should be a part of your marketing plans.

- Systematize the post-analysis of marketing research studies. This might involve, for example, the continual updating of specially-designed databases, charts, or graphs to reformat the raw BRANDS™ marketing research results into more meaningful and useful forms.

- Share marketing insights derived from particular marketing research studies with all of your BRANDS™ team members. These may require marketing research "experts" to assume coaching roles with marketing research "novices." This is a natural state of affairs. Given the complexity of BRANDS™, it is not possible to be an "expert" on everything.
- If you do not understand the workings or technical details of a specific marketing research study, review the marketing research study description in the BRANDS™ manual. If things are still unclear, consult with your course instructor. However, don't expect to receive particularly informative answers from your course instructor to broad questions of the form "Should we be ordering this marketing research study?" This sort of question is something with which you will have to struggle and ultimately resolve yourself within the context of your BRANDS™ team.

BRANDS™ Marketing Research Studies

In the rest of this chapter, each of the currently-available marketing research studies in BRANDS™ is described. Several features about these descriptions should be noted.

The current cost of executing each marketing research study is indicated in these marketing research study descriptions. Unless specifically mentioned, all marketing research studies report information based on the previous quarter (that is, the just-completed quarter).

Internal accounting records are maintained by the BRANDS™ marketing research program regarding the number of times each study has been executed by each firm. Firms are billed for the cost of these studies in the following quarter's financial and operating reports. As the example above indicates, marketing research is executed after a quarter has concluded. Therefore, the billing for this research may only be made after the following quarter's run has occurred.

Some of the marketing research studies have maximum limits associated with them. These limits represent the absolute maximum number of times each study can be executed in any quarter. These maximums reflect the finite resources of your marketing research supplier. You cannot reasonably expect that your marketing research supplier will be able to supply an unlimited number of marketing research studies during any single quarter.

Sample marketing research reports are displayed in this chapter. These sample reports are only meant to illustrate formatting and content; none of the numbers displayed in these sample reports are meant to be suggestive of actual operating policies or market situations.

An overview of all available BRANDS™ marketing research studies is provided in Table 7. The following pages in the rest of this chapter provide all of the details of these marketing research studies.

The specific numbers used to describe these BRANDS™ marketing research studies correspond to those routinely used by your marketing research supplier. There are some gaps in the sequence of marketing research numbers, corresponding to standard studies of your marketing research supplier that are not applicable to the vaporware industry in which you compete.

Table 7

OVERVIEW OF BRANDS™ MARKETING RESEARCH STUDIES

#	Marketing Research Study	Cost, Availability Limitations, and Special Notes
1	Competitive Information — Dividends and Earnings	Cost: $1,000.
2	Brand Composition Analysis	Cost: $25,000. This study may be conducted a maximum of four times per quarter.
5	Industry Sales Force Compensation	Cost: $2,500.
8	Media Content Analysis	Cost: $2,500.
11	Customer Brand Awareness	Cost: $7,000.
12	Concept Testing	Cost: $3,000 per market region. This study may be conducted a maximum of ten times per quarter.
13	Preference Testing, Two Existing Brands	Cost: $7,000 per market region. This study may be conducted a maximum of ten times per quarter.
14	Preference Testing, One Existing and One Hypothetical Brand	Cost: $14,000 per market region. This study may be conducted a maximum of ten times per quarter.
16	Operating Statistics Report	Cost: $10,000.
17	Brand Quality Ratings	Cost: $5,000.
20	Test Marketing Experiment	Cost: $50,000, $100,000, and $150,000 for one-, two-, and three-quarter test markets in any market region.
21	Brand Perceptual Ratings	Cost: $25,000.
27	Dealer Promotion Awareness	Cost: $4,000.
28	Dealer Availability	Cost: $8,000.
29	Competitive Position Audit	Cost: $50,000 per brand for brands active in only one market region, $100,000 per brand for brands active in two or more market regions. This study may be conducted a maximum of three times per quarter.
31	Industry Sales Volume Forecasts	Cost: $2,500.
32	Brand Sales Volume Forecasts	Cost: $5,000.
35	Advertising Program Experiment	Cost: $10,000 per experiment. This study may be conducted a maximum of ten times per quarter.
41	Regional Summary Analysis	Cost: $25,000 per market region.
47	Self-Reported Attribute Preferences	Cost: $5,000 per market region.

Marketing Research Study #1: Competitive Information — Dividends and Earnings

Purpose: To obtain estimates of current quarter dividends, current quarter after-tax earnings, and cumulative after-tax year-to-date earnings of a firm.

Description of the Research Process: These estimates are based on publicly available information.

Current Costs: $1,000.

Sample Study Output

```
================================================================
MARKETING RESEARCH STUDY # 1 (COMP INFO - DIVIDENDS AND EARNINGS    )
================================================================

                    CURRENT QUARTER              CUMULATIVE
                  ----------------------         YEAR-TO-DATE
                  DIVIDENDS    EARNINGS            EARNINGS
                  ---------   ----------         -----------

         FIRM 1           0    -155,440            -155,440
         FIRM 2     255,076     765,228             765,228
         ...
```

Marketing Research Study #2: Brand Composition Analysis

Purpose: To obtain the current composition of a specific vaporware brand.

Description of the Research Process: Your firm's research and development group reverse engineers the specified brand.

Current Costs: $25,000.

Availability: A maximum of four brand composition analyses may be requested in any quarter.

Other Comments: A composition analysis may be conducted only for a brand that is actively distributed in at least one BRANDS™ market region. The composition analysis is based on the brand's formulation during the last quarter, since reverse engineering can be conducted only on an existing brand. For example, if quarter "n" has just finished, and this study is executed on product 2-1, then an estimate of the brand composition of 2-1 in quarter "n" is reported. The composition of a reformulated brand is protected until the next quarter after the reformulation has taken place (that is, until the reformulated brand is actually sold on the market).

Sample Study Output

```
================================================================
MARKETING RESEARCH STUDY # 2 (BRAND COMPOSITION ANALYSIS          )
================================================================

PRODUCT 7-2 COMPOSITION:  14/45/31/ 5/ 5/5/8
```

Marketing Research Study #5: Industry Sales Force Compensation

Purpose: To obtain estimates of average sales force compensation (salary and commissions) of all firms.

Description of the Research Process: These figures are compiled by the Vaporware Industry Trade Association. Your marketing research supplier then adjusts these raw figures based on other publicly available information and their own expert judgment.

Current Costs: $2,500.

Sample
Study
Output

```
================================================================================
MARKETING RESEARCH STUDY # 5 (INDUSTRY SALES FORCE COMPENSATION          )
================================================================================

                         ALL        REGION 1     REGION 2     REGION 3
                       REGIONS      (U.S.A.  )   (EUROPE  )   (PACIFIC )
                     -----------   -----------  -----------  -----------

Salaries                2,580        2,602        2,533        2,611
Commissions               650          699          979          484
Compensation            3,230        3,301        3,512        3,095
Compensation (SD)         271          309          320          234
Commission Rate           1.8          1.7          2.0          1.5
```

Notes Regarding This Study Output: In this study output, compensation equals salaries plus commissions and "Compensation (SD)" is the standard deviation (across firms) of compensation.

Marketing Research Study #8: Media Content Analysis

Purpose: To obtain an analysis of the media content currently being employed by firms in their advertising efforts associated with each brand in all market regions in the current and previous four quarters.

Description of the Research Process: Your marketing research supplier observes and analyzes the advertising of all firms' brands.

Current Costs: $2,500.

Other Comments: Entries of "0" refer to actively-distributed brands without any advertising activity in this quarter.

```
=====================================================================
MARKETING RESEARCH STUDY # 8 (MEDIA CONTENT ANALYSIS              )
=====================================================================

                  QUARTER 45  QUARTER 46  QUARTER 47  QUARTER 48  QUARTER 49
                  ----------  ----------  ----------  ----------  ----------


REGION 1 (U.S.A.  )
  Product 1-1         10          0           0           9          10
  Product 2-2          8         10          10          15          15
  Product 4-2         10         13          13          13           5
  Product 5-2          2         20          20          19          19
  Product 6-1          1          1           1          15          15

REGION 2 (EUROPE  )
  Product 1-2          9         16          10          14          21
  Product 2-1          1          1          10           0           0
  ...
```

Marketing Research Study #11: Customer Brand Awareness

Purpose: To obtain estimates of the percentages of customers who are aware of each actively-distributed vaporware brand of all firms in all market regions for the current and previous four quarters.

Description of the Research Process: This marketing research study is based on data obtained from a customer panel operated by your marketing research supplier. The awareness of vaporware brands is evaluated with reference to the percentage of customers in the panel who identify a brand in response to the question: "Could you tell me about the brands of vaporware that you know about?" The percentage of customers who mention each brand of vaporware are defined as being aware.

Current Costs: $7,000.

Sample
Study
Output

```
=====================================================================
MARKETING RESEARCH STUDY #11 (CUSTOMER BRAND AWARENESS            )
=====================================================================

                  QUARTER 64  QUARTER 65  QUARTER 66  QUARTER 67  QUARTER 68
                  ----------  ----------  ----------  ----------  ----------


REGION 1 (U.S.A.  )
  Product 1-1        16.30       6.38        3.03       14.39       18.57
  Product 2-1        21.35      23.01       28.74       58.97       66.93
  Product 3-2        52.96      56.05       59.40       60.33       66.12
  Product 4-1        19.96      47.11       54.29       58.12       39.90
  Product 5-2        19.64      43.08       54.93       32.48       32.16
  Product 6-2        31.86      37.73       30.00       61.91       66.62

REGION 2 (EUROPE  )
  Product 1-1        35.22      13.80        5.04        2.96        2.16
  Product 1-2        69.97      49.89       74.42       73.77       83.22
  Product 2-1        73.62      71.81       74.11       41.30       16.50
  Product 3-1        27.90      19.32       54.52       64.00       62.32
  ...
```

Marketing Research Study #12: Concept Testing

Purpose: To conduct a concept test in a specified BRANDS™ market region or regions.

Description of the Research Process: This marketing research study is conducted with a representative sample of actual and potential vaporware users in the specified BRANDS™ market region. In a BRANDS™ concept test, respondents are presented with a verbal description of one possible vaporware brand, and their potential degree of interest in purchasing such a product is elicited. The respondents are asked to evaluate the proposed vaporware brand on a ten-point probability-of-purchase scale (from "absolutely no chance of purchasing" to "certain to purchase"). The percentage of respondents reporting "likely to purchase" or higher is reported. Note that this is not a usage test, since the proposed vaporware product does not have to exist.

Current Costs: $3,000 per market region.

Availability: A maximum of ten concept tests may be requested in any quarter. A concept test conducted in all BRANDS™ market regions simultaneously counts as three concept tests for the purposes of the ten concept-test-maximum per quarter.

Sample Study Output

```
========================================================================
MARKETING RESEARCH STUDY #12 (CONCEPT TESTING                          )
========================================================================

CONCEPT TESTING RESULTS FOR REGION 3 (PACIFIC ):   QUARTER 33
        CONCEPT 34/26/30/ 5/ 5/2/6 :     13.9% DEGREE-OF-INTEREST
```

Marketing Research Study #13: Preference Testing, Two Existing Brands

Purpose: To conduct a blind product preference test (including dealer prices) between two existing vaporware brands in a specified market region or regions. By definition, an existing product is one that is currently actively distributed in at least one BRANDS™ region.

Description of the Research Process: This marketing research study is conducted with a representative sample of actual and potential vaporware users in the specified market region. By executing this marketing research study, a firm receives a report of the percentage of users tested who preferred each of the two products in the test. This study involves an actual usage test of the two products.

This test is conducted on a blind basis since only the product's formulation and dealer price are at work here. The two products are repackaged in unmarked (unbranded) containers, so the users do not know which real brands the test products really are. Thus, none of the other marketing mix variables (advertising, promotion, sales force activities, and so forth) are at work in this test situation; only formulation and dealer price differ between the two tested brands. The actual execution of this study involves leaving the two products (in unlabeled packages) with the customers for a period of time and then later, after the customers have used the two products, asking them which product is most preferred. After using both products, the customers in the test are asked which they would prefer if the dealer prices of the two products were as specified. Thus, this blind product preference test isolates two of the marketing mix decision variables: product formulation and dealer price.

Current Costs: $7,000 per market region.

Availability: A maximum of ten preference tests of this type may be requested in any quarter. A preference test conducted in all BRANDS™ market regions simultaneously counts as three preference tests for the purposes of the seven preference-test-maximum per quarter.

Other Comments: A product preference test on an existing product can only be conducted for a brand that is currently being actively distributed in at least one BRANDS™ market region. This restriction exists because your marketing research supplier must purchase a quantity of these brands for use in this study.

Sample
Study
Output

```
==================================================================
MARKETING RESEARCH STUDY #13 (PREFERENCE TESTING, 2 EXISTING BRANDS   )
==================================================================

TEST RESULTS FOR REGION 1 (U.S.A.  ):  QUARTER  6 (SPRING  )
     PRODUCT 1-2,            DEALER PRICE =    880 :  12.9% PREFERENCE
     PRODUCT 5-1,            DEALER PRICE =  1,222 :  81.1% PREFERENCE
```

Marketing Research Study #14: Preference Testing, One Existing and One Hypothetical Brand

Purpose: To conduct a blind product preference test (including dealer prices) between one existing product and one hypothetical product in a specified market region or regions. By definition, an existing product is one which is currently actively distributed in at least one BRANDS™ region and a hypothetical product is any technologically valid formulation, whether available on the market now or not.

Description of the Research Process: See Marketing Research Study #13. A suitable quantity of the specified hypothetical product is created by your firm's research and development group.

Current Costs: $14,000 per market region. This cost is composed of $7,000 to create the hypothetical product in sufficient quantity to conduct the test and $7,000 to actually conduct the study.

Availability: A maximum of ten preference tests of this type may be requested in any quarter. A preference test conducted in all BRANDS™ market regions simultaneously counts as three preference tests for the purposes of the seven preference-test-maximum per quarter.

Other Comments: A product preference test on an existing product can only be conducted for a brand that is currently being actively distributed in at least one market region. This restriction exists because your marketing research supplier must purchase a quantity of these brands for use in this study.

In conducting this product preference test with a hypothetical product formulation, no reference is made to the possibility that the proposed composition of the hypothetical product might violate one or more patents if an attempt were made to actually reformulate an existing brand to have this composition. Existing patent laws do not prohibit the creation of a small quantity of a hypothetical product of the kind employed in a marketing research study of this type.

Sample
Study
Output

```
========================================================================
MARKETING RESEARCH STUDY #14 (PREFERENCE TESTING, 1 EX AND 1 HYP    )
========================================================================

TEST RESULTS FOR REGION 3 (PACIFIC ):  QUARTER 22 (SPRING  )
    PRODUCT 8-1,                 DEALER PRICE = 1,841 :  12.9% PREFERENCE
    PRODUCT  5/35/50/ 5/ 5/7/8, DEALER PRICE = 1,922 :  87.1% PREFERENCE
```

Marketing Research Study #16: Operating Statistics Report

Purpose: To obtain an Operating Statistics Report. This report contains statistics on operating ratios (usually of spending in various categories as a percentage of sales revenues). These ratios are calculated across all firms in the vaporware industry. The summary measures reported include the minimum, the mean, and the maximum for each ratio. The ratios reported include the following:
- Advertising/Revenues
- Marketing Research/Revenues
- Promotion/Revenues
- Research & Development/Revenues
- Sales Force Spending/Revenues
- Support Spending/Revenues (where Support Spending includes Advertising, Promotion, Research & Development, and Sales Force spending)
- Profits/Revenues (where Profits refers to net after-tax income)
- Sales Forecasting Accuracy Score
- Operating Efficiency Score.

These ratios are based on cumulative year-to-date financial and operating data for all firms.

Description of the Research Process: These data are derived from reports of the Vaporware Industry Trade Association.

Current Costs: $10,000.

Other Comments: In addition to displaying industry statistics, this study also reports values of the ratios for the firm requesting the study (for example, for firm #4 in the sample output shown below).

```
================================================================
MARKETING RESEARCH STUDY #16 (OPERATING STATISTICS REPORT          )
================================================================

                                             INDUSTRY NORMS
                                       ----------------------------
                               FIRM 4  MINIMUM  AVERAGE  MAXIMUM
                               ------  -------  -------  -------

ADVERTISING/REVENUES            11.2%   11.2%    11.3%    11.4%
MARKETING RESEARCH/REVENUES      0.9%    0.6%     1.0%     1.2%
PROMOTION/REVENUES               5.6%    5.6%     5.6%     5.7%
RESEARCH AND DEVELOPMENT/REVENUES 1.7%    .7%     1.9%     2.2%
SALES FORCE SPENDING/REVENUES    9.4%    9.4%     9.5%     9.5%
MARKETING SUPPORT SPENDING/REVENUES 26.9% 26.9%  27.1%    27.4%
PROFITS/REVENUES                16.5%   16.2%    16.4%    16.5%

SALES FORECASTING ACCURACY SCORE 59.6%  59.6%    77.7%    87.3%

OPERATING EFFICIENCY SCORE       5.0     3.0      4.0      5.0
```

Marketing Research Study #17: Brand Quality Ratings

Purpose: To obtain quality perception ratings of each vaporware brand.

Description of the Research Process: This study is based on a survey of vaporware users. Results are reported on a rating scale. The actual summary quality measure for each brand is the percentage of potential and actual vaporware customers who evaluated each brand to be of "good" or "excellent" quality. The actual scale used in this marketing research study is a four-point scale, where the points are described by the adjectives "poor," "fair," "good," and "excellent."

Current Costs: $5,000.

```
================================================================
MARKETING RESEARCH STUDY #17 (BRAND QUALITY RATINGS               )
================================================================

            QUARTER 19  QUARTER 20  QUARTER 21  QUARTER 22  QUARTER 23
            ----------  ----------  ----------  ----------  ----------

Product 1-1    44.80      32.40       24.43       17.53       10.39
Product 1-2    14.76      16.53       17.54       18.73       23.41
Product 2-1    54.19      29.28       37.21       51.90       41.90
Product 2-2    47.63      53.15       53.51       49.26       50.49
Product 3-1    58.73      44.89       44.98       46.38       50.94
...
```

Marketing Research Study #20: Test Marketing Experiment

Purpose: To conduct a test marketing experiment in a specified BRANDS™ market region or regions. This test marketing experiment may be one, two, or three quarters in duration.

In BRANDS™, test marketing experiments may be used to test all aspects of a brand's marketing program. Test marketing may be used to test non-design marketing program elements such as price, advertising, promotion, research and development, and sales force — either singly or in combination with each other. Test marketing may also be used to test product design variations, as well as launching currently non-active brands.

Test marketing results are received along with all other marketing research results. Test marketing results for multi-quarter tests are reported immediately. There is no time lag between ordering a multi-quarter test marketing experiment and receiving the results associated with the test marketing experiment.

Description of the Research Process: The execution of this study results in a test marketing experiment being conducted in a specified market region or regions.

Current Costs: $50,000, $100,000, and $150,000 for one-, two-, and three-quarter test markets per market region.

Sample
Study
Output

```
=================================================================================
MARKETING RESEARCH STUDY #20 (TEST MARKETING EXPERIMENT              )
=================================================================================
EXPERIMENTAL (TEST CASE) SCENARIO
TEST MARKETING RESULTS FOR PRODUCT 1-1 FOR REGION 2 (EUROPE  )
=================================================================================

                              QUARTER 10  QUARTER 11  QUARTER 12  QUARTER 13
                               [Actual]   [Forecast]  [Forecast]  [Forecast]
                              ----------  ----------  ----------  ----------

   MARKET SHARE                  51.37%      39.75%      33.87%      32.88%
   INDUSTRY SALES (Units)        98,499      90,121      93,095      93,642

 **PRICE                           500         600         600         600
   BRAND SALES (Units)           50,597      35,826      31,528      30,789
   REVENUE                   25,298,500  21,495,600  18,916,800  18,473,400
   PRODUCT COSTS              7,557,669   4,159,077   3,660,118   3,574,327
   SALES COMMISSIONS            252,985     214,956     189,168     184,734
   TRANSPORTATION             1,011,940     716,520     630,560     615,780
   GROSS MARGIN              16,475,906  16,405,047  14,436,954  14,098,559
   TOTAL FIXED COSTS          5,352,985   7,814,956   7,789,168   7,784,734
   OPERATING INCOME          11,122,921   8,590,091   6,647,786   6,313,825

 **Product Composition          5/25/60/    25/35/30/   25/35/30/   25/35/30/
                                5/ 5/5/5    5/ 5/1/2    5/ 5/1/2    5/ 5/1/2

 **Advertising Spending       2,000,000   3,500,000   3,500,000   3,500,000
 **Promotion Spending         1,000,000   2,000,000   2,000,000   2,000,000
   Res & Dev Spending           500,000     500,000     500,000     500,000
   Sales Force Salary + Commis  2,500 + 1   2,500 + 1   2,500 + 1   2,500 + 1
   Sales Force Size               100         100         100         100
   Sales Force Time Allocation   100%        100%        100%        100%
   Sales Force Spending       1,752,985   1,714,956   1,689,168   1,684,734

   Customer Brand Awareness      28.27%      33.60%      33.98%      34.16%
   Dealer Promotion Awareness    80.92%      91.05%      90.55%      90.86%
   Dealer Availability           58.86%      58.19%      53.80%      51.07%
   Product Quality Rating        69.04%      58.48%      52.93%      49.72%
   Perceived Performance           .01%        .02%        .01%        .01%
   Perceived Convenience         30.68%      12.12%      10.83%      10.90%


 *** NOTES ***
 In this test marketing experiment, OPERATING INCOME is calculated assuming
 that administrative overhead for this brand is at its base level and that
 research and development spending associated with this brand is completely
 allocated to this market region. Double asterisks ("**") to the left denote
 decision variables that have been changed in this test marketing experiment.
```

Notes Regarding This Sample Study Output: This is an example of a three-quarter test market conducted for firm #1. The just-completed quarter's actual results are shown (for reference purposes), along with the forecast values for the test marketing period. Test marketing results include both "Base Case" and "Experimental (Test Case)" scenarios, facilitating direct comparisons of the differences between the control and the experimental cases.

Other Comments: This test marketing experiment is executed in a small but representative part of the specified market region(s). The length of the test marketing experiment may be from one to three quarters. This test marketing experiment is executed using your specified test marketing decision variables and the past decision variables of all of your competitors. Your competitors will not be aware of the existence of this test marketing experiment, and they have no opportunity to intervene to attempt to influence the results of this test marketing experiment. Your competitors' marketing decision variables are held constant during the experiment at their values in the previous quarter.

Be sure to provide complete instructions for test marketing experiment changes on the Marketing Research Pre-Order Request Form. In particular, specify all brands using the normal BRANDS™ terminology. For example, brand #1 of firm #4 is described as brand 4-1. See the sample instructions below:

What marketing decision variables, if any, are to be changed prior to this test marketing experiment being conducted? Be sure to specify specific firm and brand numbers for decision variable changes.

Change advertising spending of brand 4-1 in region 2 to $2,000,000.

Change sales force time allocations in region 2 for brands 4-1 and 4-2 to 100 and 0, respectively.

Change sales force size in region 2 to 175.

Change price of brand 4-1 in region 2 to $1,005.

Marketing Research Study #21: Brand Perceptual Ratings

Purpose: To obtain product perceptual ratings of each vaporware brand along the overall perceptual dimensions of product performance and convenience.

Raw perceptual ratings are reported, as well as perceptual maps of all vaporware brands in each BRANDS™ market region. Additionally, self-reported relative importance weights for performance, convenience, and dealer price are reported.

Description of the Research Process: This study is based on a survey of potential and actual vaporware users. The performance and convenience results are reported on a six-point "terrible" to "excellent" rating scale. The actual summary perceptual measures for each brand are the percentage of survey respondents who evaluated each brand "very good" or "excellent" on each of the "performance" and "convenience" perceptual ratings scales. The self-reported importance weights are based on dividing 100 degree-of-importance points across the buying factors of performance, convenience, and dealer price.

Current Costs: $25,000.

Sample
Study
Output

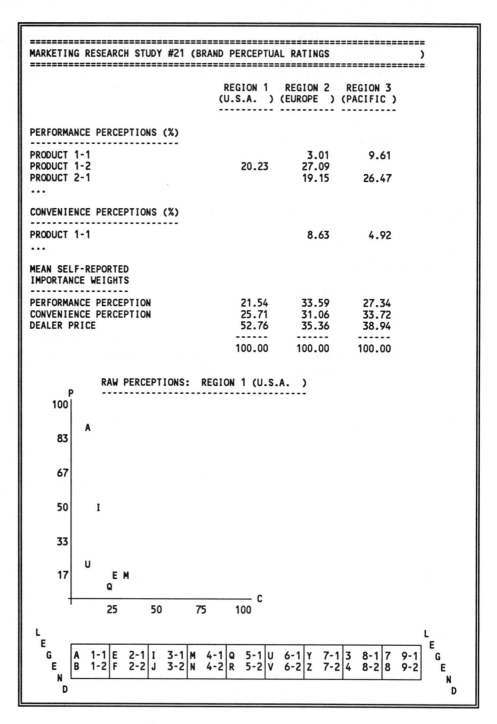

```
==============================================================================
MARKETING RESEARCH STUDY #21 (BRAND PERCEPTUAL RATINGS                        )
==============================================================================

                                        REGION 1   REGION 2   REGION 3
                                        (U.S.A.  ) (EUROPE  ) (PACIFIC )
                                        ---------- ---------- ----------

PERFORMANCE PERCEPTIONS (%)
---------------------------
PRODUCT 1-1                                           3.01       9.61
PRODUCT 1-2                               20.23      27.09
PRODUCT 2-1                                          19.15      26.47
...

CONVENIENCE PERCEPTIONS (%)
---------------------------
PRODUCT 1-1                                           8.63       4.92
...

MEAN SELF-REPORTED
IMPORTANCE WEIGHTS
------------------
PERFORMANCE PERCEPTION                    21.54      33.59      27.34
CONVENIENCE PERCEPTION                    25.71      31.06      33.72
DEALER PRICE                              52.76      35.36      38.94
                                          ------     ------     ------
                                          100.00     100.00     100.00


                RAW PERCEPTIONS:  REGION 1 (U.S.A.  )
                ------------------------------------------
      P
   100|
       |
       |   A
    83|
       |
       |
    67|
       |
       |
    50|   I
       |
       |
    33|
       |
       |   U
    17|     E M
       |   Q
       |_____ C
          25    50    75   100


 L                                                                    L
  E                                                                    E
   G  |A  1-1|E  2-1|I  3-1|M  4-1|Q  5-1|U  6-1|Y  7-1|3  8-1|7  9-1|  G
    E |B  1-2|F  2-2|J  3-2|N  4-2|R  5-2|V  6-2|Z  7-2|4  8-2|8  9-2|   E
     N                                                                 N
      D                                                                 D
```

Notes Regarding This Sample Study Output: For each market region, performance-convenience charts for raw perceptual ratings are provided. The raw performance-convenience charts display current positions of vaporware brands on performance and convenience. Of course, a third key buying factor — dealer price — is not accounted for in this raw performance-convenience chart. With regard to the scaling of the charts, natural 0%-100% scales are used in the performance-convenience charts, since performance and convenience perceptions are defined to be in the 0%-100% range by the nature of this marketing research study.

These performance-convenience charts are derived directly from the tabulations of current-quarter performance and convenience data provided at the beginning of this study's output. While containing no new information not provided elsewhere in this and other BRANDS™ marketing research studies, the visual impact of the performance-convenience charts is notable. A glance at the charts quickly reveals the leading vaporware brands and the current relative competitive standing of a specific vaporware brand.

Other Comments: Past research in the vaporware industry has indicated that product performance consists of product preference and product quality perceptions and that convenience refers to the convenience of both buying and using vaporware brands.

Marketing Research Study #27: Dealer Promotion Awareness

Purpose: To obtain estimates of the percentage of dealers who are aware of the promotion activities associated with each brand of vaporware in all market regions for the current and previous four quarters.

Description of the Research Process: These data are based on a survey of a sample of dealers in each market region. This study is conducted by the field audit staff of your marketing research supplier. Deal awareness is defined with reference to the following question posed to the sample of dealers: "Have any vaporware brands that you stock had any special promotional activity within the last quarter?" The proportion of dealers who mention each vaporware brand are defined to be aware of brand dealing (promotion) activity.

Current Costs: $4,000.

Sample
Study
Output

```
================================================================
MARKETING RESEARCH STUDY #27 (DEALER PROMOTION AWARENESS        )
================================================================

                   QUARTER 22  QUARTER 23  QUARTER 24  QUARTER 25  QUARTER 26
                   ----------  ----------  ----------  ----------  ----------

REGION 1 (U.S.A.  )
    Product 1-1       75.10        1.27         .01       65.97       50.07
    Product 2-1       69.42       61.64       72.52       72.22       63.70
    Product 3-2       61.23       64.41       63.12       69.42       83.26
    Product 4-1       73.61        1.53        9.34        9.18         .04
    Product 5-2       50.35       78.73       67.02       64.56       58.89
    Product 6-1       83.28       79.52       70.88       76.86       54.51

REGION 2 (EUROPE  )
    Product 1-2         .52         .01         .01         .01         .01
    Product 2-1       90.96       88.49       87.61       69.17       80.91
    Product 2-2       56.58       53.48       61.41         .63         .01

...
```

Marketing Research Study #28: Dealer Availability

Purpose: To obtain estimates of the percentage of dealers who sell each vaporware brand in all regions for the current and previous four quarters.

Description of the Research Process: These data are based on a survey of a sample of dealers in each market region. This study is conducted by the field audit staff of your marketing research supplier. Dealer availability refers to whether dealers currently stock a particular vaporware brand.

Current Costs: $8,000.

Sample Study Output

```
===============================================================================
MARKETING RESEARCH STUDY #28 (DEALER AVAILABILITY                             )
===============================================================================

                        QUARTER  7  QUARTER  8  QUARTER  9  QUARTER 10  QUARTER 11
                        ----------  ----------  ----------  ----------  ----------

REGION 1 (U.S.A.  )
   Product 1-1            71.92       57.79       44.50       28.97       22.58
   Product 2-2            75.02       70.02       71.25       77.00       78.27
   ...
```

Marketing Research Study #29: Competitive Position Audit

Purpose: The competitive position audit for a brand summarizes the current standing of the brand in each of the BRANDS™ market regions. Here, "current standing" is interpreted as being relative to all brands actively distributed in a market region.

Each brand's competitive position audit summarizes results for each of the BRANDS™ market regions, whether the brand is actively distributed in each region or not. Inactive brands in particular regions have blank columns of results in the audit. The elements in the competitive position audit are things that BRANDS™ participants might review to size up the current competitive market position and marketing program of a brand. The audit is really of the "checklist" variety. A wide range of marketing position statistics is examined, and the relative position of a brand (compared to all other brands currently actively distributed in the market region) is reported.

Description of the Research Process: To develop the data necessary for a competitive position audit, various other marketing research studies must be executed by your marketing research supplier.

Current Costs: $50,000 per brand for brands active in only one market region; $100,000 per brand for brands active in two or more market regions.

Availability: A maximum of three competitive position audits (for any of your brands or for competitors' brands) may be requested in any quarter.

Other Comments: The competitive position audit report attempts to summarize most (but not all) relevant marketing and financial position statistics. For each reported statistic (except things involving "Yes" or "No" answers), the brand's value is compared to the average of all brands currently actively distributed in a market region. The difference between a brand's value and the average market value is expressed in standard deviate form (in increments of 0.5 standard deviations). The relative standing of a brand on a market position statistic is then reported in standard deviate form, with the following labels being used (these label definitions appear at the bottom of the page of each brand's competitive position audit):

+ + + +	More Than 2.0 Standard Deviations Above Mean
+ + +	Between 1.5 and 2.0 Standard Deviations Above Mean
+ +	Between 1.0 and 1.5 Standard Deviations Above Mean
+	Between 0.5 and 1.0 Standard Deviations Above Mean
Average	Between -0.5 and +0.5 Standard Deviations From Mean
-	Between 0.5 and 1.0 Standard Deviations Below Mean
--	Between 1.0 and 1.5 Standard Deviations Below Mean
---	Between 1.5 and 2.0 Standard Deviations Below Mean
----	More Than 2.0 Standard Deviations Below Mean
Zero	Variable Has Value of Zero (0)
Zero&Ave	Variable Has Value of Zero (0) Which Also Equals Average

Values near the market region average (within 0.5 standard deviations of the average) are reported as being "Average." Since the value zero (0) is especially notable, a special label ("Zero") is used for any marketing position statistic that has this value. The value "Zero" overrides the usual standard deviate form of summarization. Also, if the value of a statistic is zero and the market region average is also zero, then the label "Zero&Ave" is used.

Most things reported in the competitive position audit are straight-forward and self-explanatory. The things that are novel are defined below:

- "Current" refers to the current quarter.
- "Previous" refers to the previous quarter (i.e., one quarter ago).
- "Change in Manufacturer Price?" refers to a change in manufacturer price since the previous quarter.
- "Relative Performance," "Relative Convenience," and "Relative Product Quality" all refer to perceptual measures.
- "Dealer Margin" refers to VOLUME*(PRICE*MARKUP), where VOLUME is the unit sales volume, PRICE is the manufacturer price, and MARKUP is the customary markup rate.
- "Sales Force Size" refers to the effective number of sales representatives associated with this brand in this market region (which equals sales force size times time allocation).

Even though all market regions are shown on the same page, the competitive position audit refers to comparisons involving all actively-distributed brands ("own" and competitors' brands) in each market region separately. Do not compare across regions on each page of a competitive position audit, since the "relative" calculations are based on within-region brands only.

```
================================================================
MARKETING RESEARCH STUDY #29 (COMPETITIVE POSITION AUDIT          )
================================================================

****************************************************************
COMPETITIVE POSITION AUDIT FOR PRODUCT 6-2              QUARTER 81 (WINTER )
****************************************************************

                                    REGION 1   REGION 2   REGION 3
                                    (U.S.A  )  (EUROPE )  (PACIFIC )
                                    ---------- ---------- ----------

Product Actively Distributed?          Yes        Yes        No
Current Volume Market Share          15.36       4.74       .00
Previous Volume Market Share         24.13      14.61       .00
Relative Sales Revenues                 -          -
Relative Gross Margin               Average       -
Relative Operating Income           Average    Average

Relative Distributor Price          Average    Average
Change in Manufacturer Price?          No         No
Relative Performance                    -       Average
Relative Convenience                Average    Average

Relative Product Desirability           -       Average
Relative Product Quality            Average    Average
Relative R&D Spending                   -       Average
Product Just Reformulated?             No         No

Relative Customer Awareness         Average       --
Relative Advertising Spending           -        Zero
Change in Media Content?               Yes        No
Relative Deal Awareness               ---         --
Relative Promotion Spending            --        Zero
Relative Dealer Availability            +          +
Relative Dealer Margin                 --          -
Relative Sales Force Effort         Average    Average
Relative Sales Force Size               +          -
Relative Sales Force Compens           ---         +


Legend:     ++++   More Than 2.0 Standard Deviations Above Mean
             +++   Between  1.5 and  2.0 Standard Deviations Above Mean
              ++   Between  1.0 and  1.5 Standard Deviations Above Mean
               +   Between  0.5 and  1.0 Standard Deviations Above Mean
         Average   Between -0.5 and +0.5 Standard Deviations From Mean
               -   Between  0.5 and  1.0 Standard Deviations Below Mean
              --   Between  1.0 and  1.5 Standard Deviations Below Mean
             ---   Between  1.5 and  2.0 Standard Deviations Below Mean
            ----   More Than 2.0 Standard Deviations Below Mean
            Zero   Variable Has Value of Zero (0)
        Zero&Ave   Variable Has Value of Zero (0) Which Also Equals Average
```

Marketing Research Study #31: Industry Sales Volume Forecasts

Purpose: To provide next-quarter industry sales volume forecasts for all market regions.

Description of the Research Process: These industry sales volume forecasts are based on an extrapolation of current market trends and competitive activity. These are unconditional sales volume forecasts. They assume that current marketing activities of all firms in the industry continue on their present course during the forecast period.

Current Costs: $2,500.

Sample
Study
Output

```
================================================================================
MARKETING RESEARCH STUDY #31 (INDUSTRY SALES VOLUME FORECASTS          )
================================================================================

                    QUARTER  7   QUARTER  8   QUARTER  9     QUARTER 10
                    [History]    [History]    [History]  [Forecast +/- Error]
                    ----------   ----------   ----------   --------------------

REGION 1 (U.S.A.  )   360,295      439,079      421,616    397,879 +/-  7,990
REGION 2 (EUROPE  )   281,821      310,337      294,789    276,594 +/-  4,648
REGION 3 (PACIFIC )   166,050      142,502      176,324    212,008 +/-  3,043


*** NOTE ***
"Error" corresponds to the 90% confidence interval for the forecast value.
For example, a forecast of "110,120 +/- 4,451" corresponds to a 90% degree-
of-confidence that the true value lies between 105,669 (110,120-4,451) and
114,571 (110,120+4,451).  Of course, this also implies that there is a 10%
chance that the true value will be less than 105,669 or more than 114,571.
```

Marketing Research Study #32: Brand Sales Volume Forecasts

Purpose: To provide next-quarter brand sales volume forecasts for all actively-distributed products of a firm for all market regions.

Description of the Research Process: These brand sales volume forecasts are based on an extrapolation of current market trends, seasonality, and competitive activity. These are unconditional sales volume forecasts. They assume that current marketing activities of all firms in the industry continue on their present course during the forecast period.

Current Costs: $5,000.

Sample
Study
Output

```
================================================================================
MARKETING RESEARCH STUDY #32 (BRAND SALES VOLUME FORECASTS           )
================================================================================

                    QUARTER  7   QUARTER  8   QUARTER  9     QUARTER 10
                    [History]    [History]    [History]  [Forecast +/- Error]
                    ----------   ----------   ----------   --------------------

REGION 1 (U.S.A.  )
   Product 1-1            82       18,504       21,460     24,524 +/-  1,096

REGION 2 (EUROPE  )
   Product 1-2       113,802      112,219      106,030     99,307 +/-  4,475

REGION 3 (PACIFIC )
   Product 1-1        46,609       26,771       52,397     94,647 +/-  3,991


*** NOTE ***
"Error" corresponds to the 90% confidence interval for the forecast value.
For example, a forecast of "110,120 +/- 4,451" corresponds to a 90% degree-
of-confidence that the true value lies between 105,669 (110,120-4,451) and
114,571 (110,120+4,451).  Of course, this also implies that there is a 10%
chance that the true value will be less than 105,669 or more than 114,571.
```

Marketing Research Study #35: Advertising Program Experiment

Purpose: To conduct an advertising program experiment in a specified market region. The estimated customer brand awareness associated with a specified advertising program (a combination of advertising spending level and media content for a specific product in a specific market region) is reported.

Description of the Research Process: This advertising program experiment is executed in a small but representative part of the specified market region. This advertising program experiment is executed using your advertising program and all other current marketing mix variables of your brand and all competitors' brands. Your competitors will not be aware of the existence of this advertising program experiment, and they have no opportunity to intervene to attempt to influence the results of this experiment. Competitors' marketing decision variables are held constant at their values in the previous quarter.

Current Costs: $10,000 per advertising program experiment.

Availability: A maximum of ten advertising program experiments may be requested in any quarter.

Sample Study Output

```
===================================================================
MARKETING RESEARCH STUDY #35 (ADVERTISING PROGRAM EXPERIMENT        )
===================================================================

RESULTS OF ADVERTISING EXPERIMENT FOR PRODUCT 5-2 IN REGION 2 (EUROPE ):
      Advertising Spending = $ 1,250,000
      Media Content (#)    =           21
      Estimated Customer Awareness For Product 5-2 = 50.5%
```

Marketing Research Study #41: Regional Summary Analysis

Purpose: To obtain a regional summary analysis of a variety of aggregate industry statistics and to obtain a brand performance statistics chart (volume market shares, dealer prices, and brand perception ratings) summarizing the current status of all actively-distributed brands in a specified market region.

Description of the Research Process: These estimates are based on various on-going market analyses conducted by your marketing research supplier. Average industry advertising spending, industry promotion spending, and industry average research and development spending, industry sales force sizes are compiled by the Vaporware Industry Trade Association. Aggregate market statistics are compiled from government statistical sources and by the Vaporware Industry Trade Association. These market statistics are provided to vaporware firms under an information-sharing arrangement administered by the Vaporware Industry Trade Association. Market shares are provided to vaporware firms under an information-sharing arrangement administered by the Vaporware Industry Trade Association. Dealer price data (the prices at which dealers sell vaporware brands to customers) are based on a survey of a sample of dealers in each region. This study is conducted by the field audit staff of your marketing research supplier.

Current Costs: $25,000 per market region.

```
================================================================
MARKETING RESEARCH STUDY #41 (REGIONAL SUMMARY ANALYSIS          )
================================================================


REGION STATISTICS, REGION 2 (EUROPE  ), QUARTER 44 (FALL  )
```

	Quarter		Change
	Current	Previous	(%)
Population	41,357,708	40,979,028	.9
Consumer Price Index	949	930	2.0
Per Capita Income	11,496	11,146	3.1
Industry Sales Volume	66,361	71,125	-6.7
Industry Advertising	4,000,000	8,000,000	-50.0
Industry Average D_Price	878	887	-1.0
Industry Promotion	4,000,000	3,000,000	33.3
Industry Average R&D	350,000	250,000	20.0
Industry Sales Force	350	400	-12.5

```
BRAND PERFORMANCE STATISTICS, REGION 2 (EUROPE  ), QUARTER 44 (FALL  )
```

	Volume Market Share (%)	D_Price	P_Per	P_Con
1-1	33.8 +	$ 798	57.7	27.4 ++
2-2	27.6 +	$ 842	24.3 -	21.3 ++
3-1	22.0 --	$1,028 -	11.6 -	12.9 --
4-2r	4.3 --	$1,279	58.0 +	2.9 -
6-2	12.3 --	$ 774 +	1.5 --	15.0 -

```
            0%    7%    15%    23%    31%
```

```
*** NOTES ***
(1) An "r" after a product number denotes a reformulated product in the
    just-completed quarter.
(2) Changes of more than 25%, from the previous-quarter value, are flagged
    by "++" and "--" to the right of the current-quarter entry for increases
    and decreases, respectively.  Changes of more than 5% but less than 25%,
    from the previous-quarter value, are flagged by "+" and "-" to the right
    of the current-quarter entry for increases and decreases, respectively.
    Changes of less than 5% from the previous quarter are not flagged.
(3) "D_Price" is dealer price, "P_Per" is perceived performance, and "P_Con"
    is perceived convenience.
```

Marketing Research Study #47: Self-Reported Attribute Preferences

Purpose: To provide distributions of customers' direct self-reported preferences for each vaporware raw material ingredient in a specified market region or regions.

Description of the Research Process: A representative sample of vaporware customers is asked, for each vaporware raw material ingredient, "What is your most preferred level of ... ?" The results are tabulated and reported as frequency distributions in eight categories, centered on the attribute-levels 8, 20, 32, 44, 56, 68, 80, and 92.

Current Costs: $5,000 per market region.

Other Comments: In this marketing research study output, the percentages reported for the frequencies refer to a range of attribute-levels. For example, if 13.3% (11.7%) of survey respondents report favoring a level of 20 (32) for a particular raw material, this is interpreted as corresponding to 13.3% (11.7%) of customers preferring a raw material value in the range 14.0% to 25.9% (26.0% to 37.9%).

Since Compatibility and Warranty are strictly of the "more-is-better" variety, there is no doubt about the most preferred level of these product attributes — the maximum possible level is preferred by all customers. Thus, customers' direct self-reported preferences for Compatibility and Warranty are obvious and there is no need to actually query customers about Compatibility and Warranty.

Sample
Study
Output

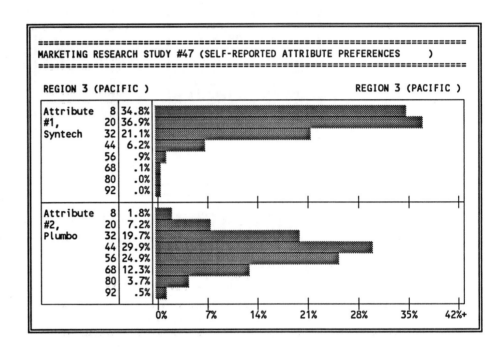

Notes Regarding This Sample Study Output: This sample study output only shows the first two attributes' results — for Syntech and Plumbo. However, this abbreviation is for space reasons only. The complete five attributes' results are reported when this marketing research study is executed.

Chapter 6

Financial and Operating Results Reports

After a game run, BRANDS™ teams receive a variety of reports. The financial and operating results reports are described and documented in this chapter. The sample financial and operating reports displayed in this chapter are only meant to illustrate formatting and content.

None of the numbers displayed in these sample reports are meant to be suggestive of actual operating policies or market situations.

Product Operating Statement and Status of Decision Variables

The first two pages of the financial and operating reports consist of a current-quarter Product Operating Statement for each vaporware brand and (at the bottom of the page) information on the current status of the brand's other decision variables. See Exhibit 1 for a sample current-quarter Product Operating Statement.

Financial results for each brand in all market regions are reported on the Product Operating Statement. Only those marketing support expenditures and other fixed costs which are unambiguously attributable to a specific brand in a specific market region are reported on the Product Operating Statement. Thus, for example, research and development expenditures for a brand are not included on the Product Operating Statement since they cannot be unambiguously allocated across the regions in which a brand is actively distributed.

On the Product Operating Statement:

- ACTIVE PRODUCT? refers to whether a brand is actively distributed in a market region.
- PRODUCT COSTS refers to per-unit cost-of-goods sold.
- SALES COMMISSIONS refers to the dollar value of sales commission.
- ADMIN O/H refers to the administrative overhead attributable to each active brand in a market region. This reflects adjustments in the base administrative overhead amount for sales volume forecasting performance.
- SALES O/H refers to the sales overhead charges, which is equal to SALES SALARIES plus SALES COMMISSIONS.

Exhibit 1

SAMPLE PRODUCT OPERATING STATEMENT REPORT

```
************************************************************************
FIRM 6:  CHAMPION VAPORWARE LIMITED
CURRENT PRODUCT OPERATING STATEMENT, PRODUCT 6-1, QUARTER 12      PAGE  1
************************************************************************
```

	ALL REGIONS	REGION 1 (U.S.A.)	REGION 2 (EUROPE)	REGION 3 (PACIFIC)
ACTIVE PRODUCT?	YES	NO	YES	YES
SALES (Units)	49,622	0	7,779	41,843
PRICE	566	570	550	570
REVENUE	28,128,960	0	4,278,450	23,850,510
PRODUCT COSTS	10,176,756	0	1,595,360	8,581,396
SALES COMMISSIONS	562,578	0	85,568	477,010
TRANSPORTATION	1,080,957	0	202,254	878,703
GROSS MARGIN	16,308,669	0	2,395,268	13,913,401
FIXED COSTS:				
ADMINISTRAT O/H	110,425	0	57,848	52,577
ADVERTISING	3,000,000	0	500,000	2,500,000
PROMOTION	502,500	0	500,000	2,500
SALES SALARIES	1,650,000	0	150,000	1,500,000
SALES O/H	2,212,578	0	235,568	1,977,010
TOTAL FIXED COSTS	7,475,503	0	1,443,416	6,032,087
OPERATING INCOME	8,833,166	0	951,852	7,881,314

```
*****************************************************
OTHER DECISION VARIABLES FOR PRODUCT 6-1 AND FIRM 6
*****************************************************
```

MEDIA CONTENT	11	7	15
SALES FORCE:			
SIZE	200	200	200
TIME ALLOCATION (%s)	0	10	100
EFFORT	.00	20.00	200.00
SALARY + COMMISSION	2,500 + 2	2,500 + 2	2,500 + 2
SALES FORECAST (Units)	0	9,000	44,000
PRODUCT COMPOSITION		53/16/21/ 5/ 5/7/2	
RESEARCH & DEVELOPMENT		240,000	

The current status of other decision variables associated with the brand are reported on the bottom of the page containing the Product Operating Statement. In the decision variable status area under the SALES FORCE subheading, EFFORT is just the product of SIZE times TIME ALLOCATION (expressed as a proportion). EFFORT is automatically calculated by the BRANDS™ software. BRANDS™ firms control only SIZE and TIME ALLOCATION. EFFORT is the equivalent number of full-time sales representatives devoting their time to supporting a particular vaporware brand in a specific BRANDS™ market region.

Divisional Operating Statement

Page three of the financial and operations report contains the current-quarter Divisional Operating Statement. This summarizes the Product Operating Statements for the individual brands as well as accounting for the various fixed costs that were not attributable to individual brands. They also include some other costs which could not be unambiguously allocated to a particular brand in a specific BRANDS™ market region. The Divisional Operating Statement is the P&L (profit and loss) statement for the vaporware division of your firm. Exhibit 2 contains a sample current-quarter Divisional Operating Statement.

  In the Divisional Operating Statement:
- CORPORATE O/H refers to corporate overhead.
- DEPRECIATION refers to the fixed depreciation component.
- INTRODUCTIONS accounts for the fixed costs of introducing a brand into a market region.
- MKTG RESEARCH refers to marketing research charges.
- REFORMULATIONS accounts for the fixed costs associated with reformulating a brand.
- SALES EXPENSES refers to the hiring and firing costs associated with changes in the size of a sales force in a market region.
- NON-OPERAT INCOME accounts for non-operating income from marketable securities (a positive contribution to income) and from loans (a negative contribution to income).

  The figures in the Divisional Operating Statement add down and across separately to the appropriate totals. However, they do not add down and across simultaneously, since some items included in the "All Products" column are not included in the individual brand columns.

Balance Sheet and Cash Flow Analysis Report

Exhibit 3 contains a sample of page four, with a firm's Divisional Balance Sheet and Cash Flow Analysis Report.

Variable Cost Calculations and Production Cost Analysis Estimates

Page five of the financial and operating results reports contains a detailed calculation of the various variable costs associated with each current vaporware brand. This detailed calculation is provided because the various components that combine to yield total variable costs of a vaporware brand are very complex. The bottom part of this page contains a Production Cost Analysis Report, which provides estimates of variable costs for the next quarter. Experience curve cost savings are reported here. Also, this report provides margin analysis calculations. See Exhibit 4 for a sample variable cost calculation and production cost analysis reports.

Exhibit 2

SAMPLE DIVISIONAL OPERATING STATEMENT REPORT

```
*************************************************************************
FIRM 8:  UNLIMITED VAPORWARE
CURRENT DIVISIONAL OPERATING STATEMENT, FIRM 8, QUARTER 21        PAGE  3
*************************************************************************

                         ALL       PRODUCT     PRODUCT
                      PRODUCTS        8-1         8-2
                     ----------- ----------- -----------

SALES (Units)            94,506      49,622      44,884

PRICE                       697         566         842

REVENUE              65,906,160  28,128,960  37,777,200
PRODUCT COSTS        31,658,540  10,176,756  21,481,784
SALES COMMISSIONS     1,318,122     562,578     755,544
TRANSPORTATION        2,262,909   1,080,957   1,181,952
                     ----------- ----------- -----------
GROSS MARGIN         30,666,589  16,308,669  14,357,920

FIXED COSTS:
  ADMINISTRAT O/H       271,190     110,425     160,765
  ADVERTISING         5,000,000   3,000,000   2,000,000
  CONSULTING FEES             0
  CORPORATE O/H         400,000
  DEPRECIATION        1,158,774
  INTRODUCTIONS         100,000           0     100,000
  MARKET RESEARCH       450,536
  PROMOTION           1,302,500     502,500   1,250,000
  REFORMULATIONS      1,000,000           0   1,000,000
  RESEARCH & DEV        850,000     500,000     350,000
  SALES EXPENSES              0
  SALES SALARIES      3,750,000   1,650,000   2,100,000
  SALES O/H           5,068,122   2,212,578   2,855,544
TOTAL FIXED COSTS    19,351,122   8,124,970  10,365,863
                     ----------- ----------- -----------
OPERATING INCOME     11,315,467   8,183,699   3,992,057
                     ----------- ----------- -----------
NON-OPERAT INCOME       400,691
LESS:  TAXES          5,858,079
                     ===========
NET INCOME            5,858,079
                     ===========
```

Other Financial and Operating Reports

Page six of the financial and operating results reports contains the details of all sales forecasting accuracy calculations, the current BRANDS™ stock market results, and operating performance summary statistics. See Exhibit 5 for a sample report.

Page seven of the financial and operating results reports contains detailed marketing research billings information. See Exhibit 6 for a sample report.

Page eight of the financial and operating results reports contains a variety of messages. See Exhibit 7 for a sample report.

Exhibit 3

SAMPLE DIVISIONAL BALANCE SHEET AND CASH FLOW ANALYSIS REPORT

```
****************************************************************************
FIRM 1:  NATIONAL VAPORWARE
DIVISIONAL BALANCE SHEET, FIRM 1, QUARTER  6                       PAGE  4
****************************************************************************


ASSETS
  CASH                                                          6,556,799
  MARKETABLE SECURITIES                                         3,626,592
  FINISHED GOODS INVENTORY                                              0
  PLANT [CAPACITY =    109,280]                                43,712,454
  TOTAL ASSETS                                                 53,895,845

LIABILITIES AND EQUITY
  LOANS                                                                 0
  INITIAL (QUARTER 0) CORPORATE CAPITALIZATION                40,000,000
  - DIVIDENDS PAID, PRIOR TO THIS YEAR                        -3,149,612
  - DIVIDENDS PAID, THIS YEAR                                 -3,798,307
  + RETAINED EARNINGS (AFTER-TAX INCOME PRIOR TO THIS YEAR)    9,448,839
  + YEAR-TO-DATE EARNINGS (AFTER-TAX INCOME THIS YEAR)        11,394,925
  TOTAL LIABILITIES AND EQUITY                                53,895,845




****************************************************************************
CASH FLOW ANALYSIS REPORT, FIRM 1, QUARTER  6                      PAGE  4
****************************************************************************


    STARTING "CASH" BALANCE (FINAL "CASH" BALANCE, QUARTER  5)  6,492,599
  + "MARKETABLE SECURITIES" (CONVERTED TO "CASH" IN QUARTER  6)   155,392
  - "LOANS" (LIQUIDATED DURING QUARTER  6)                              0
  + "FINISHED GOODS INVENTORY" INVESTMENT CHANGES                      0
  + "PLANT" INVESTMENT CHANGE (From  43,284,534 To  43,712,454)  -427,920
  + "NET INCOME"                                                5,944,979
  = INITIAL END-OF-QUARTER "CASH" BALANCE                      12,165,050
  - "DIVIDENDS" (PAID AT END OF QUARTER  6)                    -1,981,659
  = ACTUAL "CASH" BALANCE (END OF QUARTER  6)                  10,183,391
  - OPERATING "CASH" EXCESS (TO "MARKETABLE SECURITIES")       -3,626,592
  + OPERATING "CASH" DEFICIT (FROM "LOANS")                             0
  = FINAL "CASH" BALANCE (END OF QUARTER  6)                    6,556,799


*** NOTES ***
(1) "MARKETABLE SECURITIES" and "LOANS" in the second and third lines above
    refer to the values on last quarter's balance sheet.
(2) INVESTMENT CHANGEs can be positive, negative, or zero.  A positive
    (negative) {zero} INVESTMENT CHANGE corresponds to an increase (a
    decrease) {no change} in the dollar-value of the investment from last
    quarter to this quarter which leads to a decrease (an increase) {no
    change} in current-quarter "CASH" balance.
(3) In every quarter, plant capacity depreciates.  The depreciation process
    results in additions to cash, by converting investment in plant capacity
    to cash which may be used for other operating and investment purposes.
    The net "PLANT" INVESTMENT CHANGE includes this cash-increasing effect
    as well as the cash-decreasing impact of ordering new plant capacity.
(4) At most, one of OPERATING "CASH" EXCESS and OPERATING "CASH" DEFICIT will
    be non-zero; it is possible for both to be zero.  Recall that "CASH" must
    be between 8.0% and 12.0% of current-quarter sales revenues.  Excess
    "CASH" (above 12.0% of revenues) is invested in marketable securities;
    shortfalls in "CASH" (below  8.0% of revenues) result in loans.
```

Exhibit 4

SAMPLE VARIABLE COST CALCULATIONS AND PRODUCT COST ANALYSIS REPORT

```
*******************************************************************************
FIRM 3:  THREE'S COMPANY
DETAILED VARIABLE COST CALCULATIONS, FIRM 3, QUARTER 19            PAGE  5
*******************************************************************************


                                            PRODUCT  PRODUCT
                   COST COMPONENTS            3-1      3-2
-------------------------------------------  --------  --------


RAW MATERIAL #1 [SYNTECH]                       7.50    22.50
RAW MATERIAL #2 [PLUMBO]                        10.50    42.00
RAW MATERIAL #3 [GLOMP]                          4.50    13.50
RAW MATERIAL #4 [TRIMICRO]                       3.00    24.00
RAW MATERIAL #5 [FRALANGE]                       1.50     6.00
RAW MATERIAL (Experience Curve Adjust.)          0.00     0.00
LABOR (Base)                                    30.00    30.00
LABOR (Experience Curve Adjustment)             -2.06      .00
PRODUCTION (Base)                               60.00    60.00
PRODUCTION (Experience Curve Adjustment)        -4.07      .00
PACKAGING                                       10.00    10.00
VARIABLE DEPRECIATION                           24.97    24.97

SUB-TOTAL VARIABLE COSTS                       147.64   322.97

COMPATIBILITY (Cost Premium Impact)             23.62    80.74
WARRANTY (Cost Premium Impact)                  32.88    77.51

TOTAL VARIABLE COSTS                           204.14   481.22




*******************************************************************************
PRODUCT COST ANALYSIS ESTIMATES, FIRM 3, QUARTER 19                 PAGE  5
*******************************************************************************

                   ESTIMATES OF NEXT QUARTER
                   EXPERIENCE CURVE ADJUSTED
                   VARIABLE (Per Unit) COSTS          MARGIN ANALYSIS
                   --------------------------------   ============================

                    RAW    PDCOST  PROD
                   MATERI  +PKCST  +LABOR   TOTAL     PRICE     COST    MARGIN
                   ------  ------  ------  --------   --------  --------  --------

PRODUCT 3-1        27.00   34.44   80.26   195.93     566.00    195.93   370.07
PRODUCT 3-2       108.00   34.44   90.00   346.34     850.00    346.34   503.66


*** NOTES ***
(1) The variable depreciation cost (PDCOST) figure in this table has been
    estimated under the assumption that production next quarter is equal to
    plant capacity.
(2) In this table, PKCST refers to packaging cost.
(3) MARGIN ANALYSIS figures do not include transportation and shipping costs.
(4) TOTAL includes cost-premium impacts of Compatibility and Warranty.
```

Exhibit 5

SAMPLE SALES FORECASTING ACCURACY, STOCK MARKET REPORT AND OPERATING PERFORMANCE SUMMARY REPORTS

```
****************************************************************************
FIRM 4:  NORTH AMERICAN VAPORWARE
SALES FORECASTING ACCURACY REPORT, FIRM 4, QUARTER  6              PAGE  6
****************************************************************************

            MARKET      SALES       ACTUAL      ACCURACY
PRODUCT     REGION     FORECAST      SALES        SCORE
-------     ------     --------     -------     --------


 4-1          2          9,000       7,779        84.30
 4-1          3         44,000      41,843        94.85
 4-2          1         50,000      41,142        78.47
 4-2          2         20,000       3,742          .00
AVERAGE (Current Quarter)                         53.54

ON   7 SALES VOLUME FORECASTS IN THE CURRENT YEAR:
     CUMULATIVE (Total) FORECASTING SCORE POINTS =   374.77
     AVERAGE FORECASTING SCORE (Per Forecast)   =    53.54


*** NOTE ***
Only forecasts associated with actual market shares of at least  2.5% in a
market region are counted in the calculation of forecasting accuracy scores.




****************************************************************************
STOCK MARKET REPORT, FIRM 4, QUARTER  6                            PAGE  6
****************************************************************************


CURRENT STOCK PRICE (Per Share), FIRM 1   $    80 1/2
CURRENT STOCK PRICE (Per Share), FIRM 2   $    66 1/2
CURRENT STOCK PRICE (Per Share), FIRM 3   $    96 1/8
CURRENT STOCK PRICE (Per Share), FIRM 4   $   137 5/8
...




****************************************************************************
OPERATING PERFORMANCE SUMMARY REPORT, FIRM 4, QUARTER  6          PAGE  6
****************************************************************************

                                                      MARKET SHARES (%)
                                                      -----------------
                  REVENUES ($)   EARNINGS ($)  ROI (%)  VOLUME   DOLLAR
                  ------------   ------------  -------  -------  -------

CURRENT QUARTER    84,980,160     1,724,930     11.5    50.20    50.20
PREVIOUS QUARTER   88,136,820     2,097,795     14.0    50.69    50.69
CHANGE RATE            -3.6%        -17.8%     -17.8%    -1.0%    -1.0%
```

Exhibit 6

SAMPLE MARKETING RESEARCH BILLINGS REPORT

```
**********************************************************************
FIRM 2:  CRASH-AND-BURN VAPORWARE LTD.
MARKETING RESEARCH BILLINGS, FIRM 2, QUARTER  5              PAGE  7
**********************************************************************


STUDY                                      UNIT
  #     MARKETING RESEARCH STUDY DESCRIPTION  COST   TIMES   COST
-----   ------------------------------------ -------  ------- ---------

   1    COMP INFO - DIVIDENDS AND EARNINGS    1,000      4    4,000
   5    INDUSTRY SALES FORCE COMPENSATION     5,000      1    5,000
  16    OPERATING STATISTICS REPORT          25,000      1   25,000
  17    BRAND QUALITY RATINGS                 7,000      1    7,000
  28    DEALER AVAILABILITY                   8,000      1    8,000
  31    INDUSTRY SALES VOLUME FORECASTS       2,000      1    2,000
  32    BRAND SALES VOLUME FORECASTS          4,000      1    4,000
  55    INFORMATION SYSTEMS COSTS {PAGE COUNTS}  1,000  15   15,000

TOTAL                                                      70,000


*** NOTE ***
This marketing research billing report is based on marketing research ordered
after BRANDS quarter  4 and billed in connection with BRANDS quarter 5.
```

Exhibit 7

SAMPLE FINANCIAL AND OPERATING STATEMENT MESSAGES REPORT

```
**********************************************************************
FIRM 9:  PHOENIX VAPORWARE
FINANCIAL AND OPERATING STATEMENT MESSAGES, FIRM 9, QUARTER 22     PAGE  8
**********************************************************************


PRODUCT FORMULATION STATUS
    Product 9-1 has formulation 20/50/20/ 5/ 5/1/8.
    Product 9-2 has formulation 30/30/30/ 5/ 5/7/4.

VAPORWARE TECHNOLOGY CONSTRAINTS
    Product attributes #1-#5 must sum to exactly 100.
    Attribute #4 [Trimicro    ] must equal   5.
    Attribute #5 [Fralange    ] must equal   5.

SALES FORECASTING ACCURACY SCORES
    Product 9-1, region 2, sales forecasting accuracy is very poor [   .00].
    Product 9-2, region 3, sales forecasting accuracy is very poor [ 25.47].

REGIONAL GROSS MARGINS
    All products in all regions have contribution margins greater than 25%.

SPECIAL NOTES, REMINDERS, AND WARNING MESSAGES
    Product 9-2 reformulated to 30/30/30/ 5/ 5/7/4.
```

Chapter 7

Performance Evaluation in BRANDS™

Each team's performance in BRANDS™ is evaluated on the basis of three general criteria — financial performance, market performance, and operating efficiency. The challenge facing each BRANDS™ team is to maximize long-run profitability, given the initial starting situation. Overall performance evaluation in BRANDS™ is based on assessing of the extent to which each team fulfills this mandate. This chapter describes a quantitative performance evaluation methodology which combines measures of financial performance, market performance, and operating efficiency.

Financial Performance

Financial performance could, in principle, be measured in a number of ways. Current financial performance and trends in financial performance are both relevant. Long-term financial performance and potential are key. Attempts to achieve attractive short-term financial results at the possible expense of long-term financial performance should be viewed unfavorably.

Absolute earnings in a BRANDS™ year is an obvious performance measure. More important, however, is ROI (return on investment). In BRANDS™, "investment" includes both common stock and cumulative retained earnings to date, since these are the funds to which a firm has access during a BRANDS™ year. Thus, as used here, ROI is a measure of return on equity. For example, suppose that a BRANDS™ firm had a corporate investment of $120 million and cumulative retained earnings of $30 million at the end of year 4. For this firm, "Investment" is then $150 million. Assume that the firm pays no dividends during BRANDS™ year 5. Then, new after-tax earnings of $27 million in year 5 would represent an after-tax ROI of 27/150 = 18%.

Since your vaporware firm has publicly traded stock, stock price might be viewed as a relevant measure of financial performance. Stock price presumably reflects current and recent-past financial performance, since expectations about future earnings potential presumably are based largely on current and recent-past earnings levels.

ROI is the specific financial measure used in the BRANDS™ quantitative performance valuation mechanism.

Market Performance

Market performance is closely related to market share. Current market share and trends in market share through time are both relevant, however.

Market share may be reasonably interpreted as representing future earnings potential, hence its relevance in performance evaluation. Note, however, that market share may easily be manipulated in the short-run by an individual firm. For example, market share may be "bought" or "sold" at the expense or benefit of long-term profitability. Attention to trends is crucial to the successful interpretation of the strength of a market-share position.

Change in market share from year to year is the specific market performance evaluation measure used in the BRANDS™ quantitative performance evaluation mechanism.

Operating Efficiency

Operating efficiency is important in any industry so that needless costs are not incurred. In general, an efficiently run firm would:
- forecast sales well
- spend relatively modest amounts on support (advertising, research and development, promotion, and sales force)
- achieve a high level of profitability relative to sales revenue

While poor performance on any of these ultimately leads to increased costs which reduces profitability, many other things affect profitability as well. Thus, it seems desirable to explicitly develop a measure of operating efficiency and to reward firms, at least partially, based on their operating efficiency.

In BRANDS™, each firm is evaluated on operating efficiency as well as on financial (return on investment) and market (change in market share) performance criteria. Since operating efficiency must be gauged relative to competitors' levels, relative standing on these measures is the determinant of operating efficiency. In particular, operating efficiency is determined as follows in BRANDS™:

Operating Efficiency = Sales Forecasting Efficiency
+ Spending Support Efficiency
+ Profitability Efficiency.

These operating efficiency components are defined in Table 8.

After calculating each operating efficiency component, the number of points in "Weight" in Table 8 is awarded to each firm when its component value is less than (or more than, for measures where "more-is-better") to another firm's corresponding value. Thus, with n firms in an industry, the best-performing firm on this component receives a score of n-1 points times "Weight." The worst performing firm receives zero points. Each efficiency measure is equal to the number of points achieved in these comparisons. Thus, Operating Efficiency is an index in which higher values are better than lower values. This index has a minimum possible value of zero, if a firm is worst on all of the components of OPERATING EFFICIENCY, and a maximum value of 4(n-1) for an n-firm industry, if a firm is best on all of the components of Operating Efficiency.

Table 8

OPERATING EFFICIENCY COMPONENTS AND WEIGHTS

Component	Definition	Weight
Sales Forecasting	Compare sales volume forecasts to actual sales volumes. For each forecast, a forecasting score is developed based on awarding 100 points to a forecast that is within 1% of actual, 99 points to a forecast that is within 2% of actual, and so on. Thus, the average forecasting score indicates how close a firm typically forecasts sales compared to actual. For example, an average forecast score of 90 indicates that the firm typically forecasts sales volumes within 10% of actual levels. [*More is better.*]	1
Support Spending	Marketing support spending (on advertising, promotion, research and development, and sales force) across all brands and all regions to sales revenues. [*Less is better.*]	1
Profitability	After-tax profits divided by sales revenues. [*More is better.*]	2

Sales Forecasting Efficiency is a particularly pure correlate of market understanding and insight, and thus of operating efficiency. Note that good Sales Forecasting Efficiency presumably leads to efficient management of inventories and capacities. Profitability Efficiency receives a weight of two because it reflects overall profit and cost management. Note, however, that Profitability Efficiency can be influenced unduly by a firm that is "selling off" (harvesting) market share to achieve short-run profitability, even at the expense of long-run profitability. Thus, this variable is not a completely pure measure of operating efficiency. However, it has considerable relevance, hence its weight of two.

BRANDS™ Quantitative Performance Evaluation

The BRANDS™ quantitative performance evaluation mechanism is designed to provide a purely quantitative measure of performance in the simulation exercise. Presumably, other evaluation procedures may be used as well (written marketing plans, performance relative to specific goals, etc.).

In the first BRANDS™ year, ROI, operating efficiency, and change in market share each have an overall weighting of one. After the first year, the weighting doubles. Also, after the first year, year-over-year change in each has a weighting of one.

A sample BRANDS™ quantitative performance evaluation report is shown in Exhibit 8. Cumulative Points are translated automatically into a "Grade" which ranges from 70%-100% with a mean of 85%.

Exhibit 8

SAMPLE BRANDS™ QUANTITATIVE PERFORMANCE EVALUATION REPORT

	Firm 1	Firm 2	Firm 3	Firm 4
Quarter 1 OE	21.0	21.0	21.0	21.0
Quarter 2 OE	31.0	25.0	6.0	22.0
Quarter 3 OE	29.5	14.0	9.0	31.5
Quarter 4 OE	29.5	8.5	14.0	32.0
Year 1, Total OE	111.0	68.5	50.0	106.5
Year 1, OE Points	3.0	1.0	.0	2.0
Year 1, ROI%	13.3	4.2	10.9	17.3
Year 1, ROI% Points	2.0	.0	1.0	3.0
Market Share Change	1.9	-2.5	-.6	1.2
Market Share Change Points	3.0	.0	1.0	2.0
Year 1, Total Points	8.0	1.0	2.0	7.0
Cumulative Points	8.0	1.0	2.0	7.0
Quarter 5 OE	13.0	23.0	25.0	23.0
Quarter 6 OE	13.0	27.0	13.0	31.0
Quarter 7 OE	5.0	26.0	24.0	29.0
Year 2, Total OE	31.0	76.0	62.0	83.0
Year 2, OE Points	.0	4.0	2.0	6.0
OE Change	-80.0	7.5	12.0	-23.5
OE Change Points	.0	2.0	3.0	1.0
Year 2, ROI%	-14.6	42.1	7.3	22.9
Year 2, ROI% Points	.0	6.0	2.0	4.0
ROI% Change	-27.9	37.9	-3.7	5.6
ROI% Change Points	.0	3.0	1.0	2.0
Market Share Change	-8.3	4.3	-7.6	11.7
Market Share Change Points	.0	4.0	2.0	6.0
Year 2, Total Points	.0	19.0	10.0	19.0
Cumulative Points	8.0	20.0	12.0	26.0
Overall Grade (Mean=85%)	77%	88%	81%	94%

Chapter 8

Decision Making Logistics and Related Paperwork

To make changes in current marketing and non-marketing decisions in BRANDS™, firms must complete appropriate decision change forms and submit these forms to the BRANDS™ Game Administrator. The BRANDS™ Game Administrator ensures that the changes are made prior to the next game run. There are specific decision change forms in BRANDS™. These forms are included in this chapter.

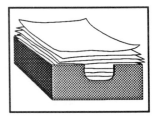

All decision variable changes are of the form "make this decision equal to ... ," *not* "change this decision by this much ... ."

To request marketing research studies, you must complete marketing research study request forms. The multi-page marketing research study request form is included in this chapter. Marketing research is executed after the next game run, so marketing research results reflect the most recent quarter's activities.

Note that the various product development and testing marketing research requests that require a "price" to be associated with existing or proposed vaporware formulations refer to "dealer price," *not* "manufacturer price." The key here is that the relevant "price" is the price seen by the customer in the context of the marketing research study.

These forms, for decision changes and for marketing research, must be submitted no later than the announced time for each decision period. Decision change forms submitted after this deadline may not be entered into the BRANDS™ database in time to take effect with the next quarter.

Photocopy these various BRANDS™ forms (on pages 66-70), as necessary, to use throughout the BRANDS™ exercise. **Permission is hereby granted without charge, royalty, or copyright payment to anyone wishing to making photocopies of pages 66-70 for use during a BRANDS™ exercise.** Since the BRANDS™ participant's manual is copyrighted, you may need to show this photocopying permission statement to a commercial copy shop to facilitate photocopying of multiple copies of pages 66-70.

Remember, all BRANDS™ decisions are "permanent." That is, BRANDS™ decisions stay the same from quarter to quarter until they are explicitly changed. Thus, only changes need to be entered on these decision variable change forms.

Marketing Decision Variables Change Form

Firm#-Brand#	—	Quarter#

	Region #1 (U.S.A.)	Region #2 (Europe)	Region #3 (Pacific)
Introduce or Drop This Brand?			
Manufacturer Price [$/unit]			
Advertising [$]			
Media Content [#]			
Promotion [$]			
Sales Forecast [units]			

Research and Development Spending [$]	

Reformulation Request	Formulation:

General Notes and Reminders

(1) Only enter items for which changes are required.

(2) "Special KTM" numbers may be used in this Marketing Decision Variables Change Form. For example, 3,000,000 may be designated as 3M (where "M" means millions), 2,200,000 may be designated as 2.2M, and 23,000 may be designated as 23K or 23T (where "K" and "T" means thousands).

(3) When "Dropping a Brand From Active Distribution": You must also change your marketing support spending levels to zero (for advertising and promotion) and reallocate your sales force time allocation from dropped brands to actively-distributed brands.

Sales Force Decision
Variable Change Form

Firm# [   ]   Quarter# [   ]

	Region #1 (U.S.A.)	Region #2 (Europe)	Region #3 (Pacific)
Sales Force Salary [$ per person per month]			
Sales Force Commission Rate [% of revenues]			
Sales Force Size [# of representatives]			
Sales Force Time Allocations [%s] — Brand #1			
Sales Force Time Allocations [%s] — Brand #2			
	100%	100%	100%

General Notes and Reminders

(1) Only enter items for which changes are required, except for sales force time allocations where numbers must be entered for all brands in any market region in which sales force time is reallocated across brands.

(2) When changing sales force time allocations, enter time allocations for all brands. Time allocations must sum to 100% in each market region. If any of these time allocations are 0%, be sure to enter the value 0 (zero).

(3) "Special KTM" numbers may be used in this Sales Force Decision Variables Change Form. For example, 3,000,000 may be designated as 3M (where "M" means millions), 2,200,000 may be designated as 2.2M, and 23,000 may be designated as 23K or 23T (where "K" and "T" means thousands).

Marketing Research Pre-Order Request Form

Firm#		Quarter#	

1	Competitive Information - Dividends and Earnings	Firm #s:		
2	Brand Composition Analysis	Firm#s—Brand#s (max. of 4):		
5	Industry Sales Force Compensation			
8	Media Content Analysis			
11	Customer Brand Awareness			

12	Concept Testing (*Note:* *If a concept test is required for all market regions, enter "A" as the market region number.*)	Region(s):	Formulation:
		Region(s):	Formulation:
		Region(s):	Formulation:
		Region(s):	Formulation:
		Region(s):	Formulation:
		Region(s):	Formulation:
		Region(s):	Formulation:
		Region(s):	Formulation:
		Region(s):	Formulation:
		Region(s):	Formulation:

13	Preference Testing, Two Existing Brands (*Note: "Price" refers to dealer price, the price at which final customers purchase vaporware brands. A dealer price must be provided for each brand, even if the dealer price is to be the same for both formulations. If a preference test is required for all market regions, enter "A" as the market region number.*)	Region(s):	Price:	Firm#-Brand#:
			Price:	Firm#-Brand#:
		Region(s):	Price:	Firm#-Brand#:
			Price:	Firm#-Brand#:
		Region(s):	Price:	Firm#-Brand#:
			Price:	Firm#-Brand#:
		Region(s):	Price:	Firm#-Brand#:
			Price:	Firm#-Brand#:
		Region(s):	Price:	Firm#-Brand#:
			Price:	Firm#-Brand#:

		Region(s):	Price:	Firm#-Brand#:
			Price:	Firm#-Brand#:
		Region(s):	Price:	Firm#-Brand#:
			Price:	Firm#-Brand#:
		Region(s):	Price:	Firm#-Brand#:
			Price:	Firm#-Brand#:
		Region(s):	Price:	Firm#-Brand#:
			Price:	Firm#-Brand#:
14	Preference Testing, One Existing Brand and One Hypothetical Brand	Region(s):	Price:	Firm#-Brand#:
			Price:	Formulation:
		Region(s):	Price:	Firm#-Brand#:
			Price:	Formulation:
	(Note: "Price" refers to dealer price, the price at which final customers purchase vaporware brands. A dealer price must be provided for each brand and formulation, even if the dealer price is to be the same for both formulations. If a preference test is required for all market regions, enter "A" as the market region number.)	Region(s):	Price:	Firm#-Brand#:
			Price:	Formulation:
		Region(s):	Price:	Firm#-Brand#:
			Price:	Formulation:
		Region(s):	Price:	Firm#-Brand#:
			Price:	Formulation:
		Region(s):	Price:	Firm#-Brand#:
			Price:	Formulation:
16	Operating Statistics Report			
17	Brand Quality Ratings			
20	Test Marketing Experiment *(Note: If a test marketing experiment is required for all market regions, enter "A" as the market region number.)*	Region(s): Test Market Length (max. of 3 Qs): What marketing decision variables, if any, are to be changed prior to this test marketing experiment being conducted?		

21	Brand Perceptual Ratings			
27	Dealer Promotion Awareness			
28	Dealer Availability			
29	Competitive Position Audit	Firm#s—Brand#s (max. of 4):		
31	Industry Sales Volume Forecasts			
32	Brand Sales Volume Forecasts			
35	Advertising Program Experiment	Region:	Advertising Spending:	Media Content:
		Region:	Advertising Spending:	Media Content:
		Region:	Advertising Spending:	Media Content:
		Region:	Advertising Spending:	Media Content:
		Region:	Advertising Spending:	Media Content:
		Region:	Advertising Spending:	Media Content:
		Region:	Advertising Spending:	Media Content:
		Region:	Advertising Spending:	Media Content:
		Region:	Advertising Spending:	Media Content:
		Region:	Advertising Spending:	Media Content:
41	Regional Summary Analysis	Region(s):		
47	Self-Reported Attribute Preferences	Region(s):		

General Notes on Pre-Ordering Marketing Research Studies

(1) To pre-order marketing research, circle the appropriate marketing research study numbers on the left side of this request form. If a marketing research study requires additional specific details, provide the specifics in the boxes to the right.

(2) Some marketing research studies may be executed simultaneously in all market regions. To order marketing research studies in all market regions simultaneously, request market region "A" when pre-ordering.

(3) "Special KTM" numbers may be used in this Marketing Research Pre-Order Request Form. For example, 3,000,000 may be designated as 3M (where "M" means millions), 2,200,000 may be designated as 2.2M, and 23,000 may be designated as 23K or 23T (where "K" and "T" means thousands).

Chapter 9

The BRANDS™ Disk

> *Note:* *This chapter describes topics and features that are optional within BRANDS™. Your course instructor will advise you if the material in this chapter is to be used in your particular BRANDS™ exercise.*

The BRANDS™ decision variable change forms on pages 66-70 are used to record your decision variable changes and marketing research pre-order requests. Someone must enter the requests on the BRANDS™ forms into the BRANDS™ data base. In some circumstances, the course instructor arranges to have this data entry task handled for you. However, it is also possible to "do it yourself" using the BRANDS™ software described in this chapter. By entering your own data, you take complete control over your own destiny. Data entry errors, for example, are fully within your own control.

Introduction

All decision variable changes are entered into the BRANDS™ data base via the B_INPUT program. This program is on the BRANDS™ participant's disk. Marketing research requests are also pre-ordered using program B_INPUT. The course instructor may require or suggest that the usual BRANDS™ decision variable change forms and marketing research request forms (i.e., those  contained in the BRANDS™ manual) be submitted along with the BRANDS™ participant's disk.

Pre-ordered marketing research studies are not executed at the time of pre-ordering. Rather, all necessary marketing research study parameters and specifications are recorded by the B_INPUT program. Later, after the next BRANDS™ game run, these parameters and specifications are used to execute the pre-ordered marketing research studies.

The BRANDS™ participant's disk contains the BRANDS™ B_INPUT program, all data files used by the B_INPUT program, and all updated financial and marketing research results files after each BRANDS™ game run. Due to the size of these files, there is little or no room for any other "personal" (not generated by the BRANDS™ software) files on this disk.

Only this single disk is needed for all BRANDS™ activities. To use this disk, an IBM

PC/XT/AT/386/486 or "100%"-compatible clone, running under PC- or MS-DOS (Versions 2.10 or later), is required. This machine must have at least 384K of free RAM after loading DOS and at least one disk drive.

General Instructions For Program B_INPUT

In what follows, things that are typed at the keyboard are *bolded and italicized*. As with all PC programs, after typing any numerical entry, you need to press the *<Enter>* key to have the program process your entry.

Menus in B_INPUT require you to use the cursor keys to select a menu element, and then press *<Enter>* to execute your actual choice. If you press *<Esc>* while at a menu, you will immediately terminate your current activities and branch to the next higher menu level.

At some points in B_INPUT, you will be prompted to enter a number. For example, you may be asked to input the number of a particular product or market region. To terminate processing of any B_INPUT program command part-way through this input process, press *<Esc>*. Processing of the current command then terminates immediately and program control passes to the next higher level of the B_INPUT program.

When inputing numerical values in B_INPUT, "special KTM" numbers may be used. For example, input of *2M* is interpreted as the value 2,000,000. Similarly, the input of *2.7K* or *2.7T* is interpreted by B_INPUT as the value 2,700.

When entering regular and "special KTM" numbers, do not use commas. That is, enter *2000000* not 2,000,000. Of course, a shorter, faster, and less error-prone way to enter *2000000* is by entering this value as *2M*. Small or capital letter versions of "K" and "M" may both be used.

When You Receive the BRANDS™ Disk

When you receive the BRANDS™ participant's disk, the following DOS files must be on it: B_INPUT.EXE, INDUSTRY.DAT, DVn.BIN, DVPARAMn.BIN, and PREMRSn.BIN, where "n" refers to your firm number. These files must always be on the BRANDS™ disk. Other files are created along the way by the B_INPUT program.

The contents of these files are described later in this documentation. If these files are not on your disk, contact your course instructor immediately.

To list the contents of a disk, type *DIR* at the DOS prompt.

Starting and Running Program B_INPUT

To start program B_INPUT:

[1] Boot-up the PC. If you are using a hard disk machine, turn the machine on. If you are using a two-disk drive machine with no hard disk, place a copy of a disk which contains the operating system in the A: drive and then turn on the machine. During the boot-up phase, the operating system may ask for the date and the time. Just hit the *<Enter>* key twice; it isn't necessary to enter a date and time. You should now be at the A> prompt.

[2] Put the BRANDS™ disk in the A: drive. If you are using a hard disk machine, make the A: drive the default drive by typing *A: .*

[3] Type **_B_INPUT_** to initiate the execution of BRANDS™ program B_INPUT. Press the **_<Enter>_** key or any other key to continue on from the BRANDS™ introductory identification screen.

The B_INPUT program's main menu, shown below, then appears:

Program B_INPUT: Main Menu
Change Decision Variables Forecast Current Product Operating Statements, Next Quarter
Process Marketing Research Study Pre-Order Requests Set Current MR Study Pre-Orders To Equal Previous MR Study Pre-Orders Cancel All Pre-Ordered Marketing Research Studies
Immediate Update of Decision Variable and Marketing Research Files
Change Decision Variables For Test Marketing Experiment (MR Study #20)
Exit Program B_INPUT Without Saving Any Changes (Abnormal Exit)
Save Files and Exit Program B_INPUT

Select an Option Using the Cursor Keys and Then Press the <Enter> Key,
or Press <Esc> To Quit (Which Automatically Saves All Files)

The current menu item is always shown in reverse video. Use the cursor keys to identify the desired menu item, and then press **_<Enter>_** to select it.

In the main menu shown above:

- **Change Decisions Variables** leads to a series of screens that permit you to change your current decisions variables. When you complete changing decision variables, B_INPUT "checks" all current decision variables for logical consistency. Unusual situations are flagged and displayed on the screen and also written to an ASCII-text file, MESSAGES.DAT, on the BRANDS™ disk. After "checking" decision variables, you should review any things flagged to ensure that the flagged entries are as you really want them to be. "Checking" does not check all possible logical relationships, nor can it read your mind with regard to what you meant to input. However, it identifies some obvious problem areas, if they exist.

- **Forecast Current Product Operating Statements, Next Quarter** leads to a series of screens which provide forecasted profit-and-loss statements for the next quarter, based on your current decision variable input. These forecasts are based on a restrictive set of assumptions, which are shown on a general information screen that is displayed when you first select this menu item.

- **Process Marketing Research Study Pre-Order Requests** leads to a sub-menu that has options allowing you to execute, cancel, or display the status of marketing research study pre-orders.

- **Set Current MR Study Pre-Orders To Equal Previous MR Study Pre-Orders** results in the current marketing research study pre-orders being set equal to their values as of the previous quarter.

- **Cancel All Pre-Ordered Marketing Research Studies** results in all marketing research study pre-orders being canceled.

- **Immediate Update of Decision Variable and Marketing Research Files** does just what it says. Note that all of these files are automatically saved to disk when you exit B_INPUT either through the **Save Files and Exit BRANDS™ Program B_INPUT** menu selection or by pressing the *<Esc>* key. If you are making a lot of decision variable and marketing research study pre-order changes, you may wish to return to the main menu and execute **Immediate Update of Decision Variable and Marketing Research Files** periodically.

- **Change Decision Variables For Test Marketing Experiment (MR Study #20)** leads to a series of screens that permit you to change your current decision variables for a test marketing experiment. These test marketing decision variable changes are only in effect during a test marketing experiment; they do not affect your current decision variables in any way.

- **Exit BRANDS™ Program B_INPUT Without Saving Any Changes (Abnormal Exit)** exits program B_INPUT without saving any of the changes that have been made in this particular usage occasion.

- **Save Files and Exit BRANDS™ Program B_INPUT** exits program B_INPUT. All relevant files are automatically updated and saved to disk during this exit procedure. You may also exit B_INPUT by pressing *<Esc>*.

Changing Decision Variables

Only changes in decision variables must be entered via program B_INPUT. Decision variables which do not change from one quarter to the next do not have to be entered. Unless changed, all decision variables from the previous quarter are still in effect in, and carry over to, the next quarter.

Spreadsheet-style inputing exists in BRANDS™ program B_INPUT. This includes screens that display the current values of decision variables, permit you to use the cursor keys to move around a screen, and select a specific decision variable to change. When you have located the cursor on the particular data element you wish to change, you just start typing in the new value. By pressing *<Enter>* or any other cursor control key after typing the last digit of your entry, the new value is recorded in the BRANDS™ data base. As the new value is recorded in the BRANDS™ data base, it is also displayed in the appropriate field on your screen.

Follow the instructions on the decision variable change screens. For ease of reference, current decision variable values are shown on the various spreadsheets. You do not have to re-enter these values.

With the cursor in a particular spreadsheet cell (highlighted in reverse video):

- If you press a number (0-9), it is presumed that you wish to update this cell's value. Continue to type the rest of the number's digits, concluding with a cursor control key (such as *<Enter>* or *<Cursor-Down>*). When a cursor control key is encountered, B_INPUT processes your update (and checks to see that you have entered a valid number, within the appropriate BRANDS™ upper and lower bounds) and then move to the cell indicated by your cursor control key. Concluding your entry with *<Enter>* automatically moves you one cell to the right. To move down the spreadsheet, conclude your data entry with *<Cursor-Down>*.

- If you press a cursor control key (such as *<PgUp>*, *<PgDn>*, *<Enter>*, *<Cursor-Up>*, *<Cursor-Right>*, *<Cursor-Left>*, or *<Cursor-Down>*), it is presumed that you wish to move to another spreadsheet cell. Note that cursor control keys *<Home>* and *<End>* result in immediate movement to the upper-right and lower-left cells on the spreadsheet, respectively.

When using BRANDS™ program B_INPUT, a signalling feature permits users to quickly identify which decision variables have been changed. Flashing symbols after each decision variables are associated with changed values. Here, "changed" means a value different from the value which existed immediately after the last game run. In particular:

- A flashing "+" after an entry denotes that this decision variable has been changed and increased from the value that existed immediately after the last game run.
- A flashing "-" after an entry denotes that this decision variable has been changed and decreased from the value that existed immediately after the last game run.
- A flashing "c" after an entry denotes that this decision variable has been changed from the value that existed immediately after the last game run. This symbol is used for decision variables where "increases" and "decreased" are not meaningful (e.g., introductions and media content).

Enter all of your changes in BRANDS™ decision variables, as required. All decision variable changes are entered via the B_INPUT program.

It is possible to reset decision variables to their "original" values. Here, "original" refers to the values that existed immediately after the last game run. To reset a decision variable, move the cursor to the desired spreadsheet element (corresponding to the decision variable that you wish to reset) in B_INPUT and immediately strike the *<BackSpace>* key. Follow the subsequent on-screen instructions to complete the reset operation. (Incidentally, if the cursor is on any position but the first within a cell in the various B_INPUT spreadsheets, the *<BackSpace>* key does not perform a reset operation. Rather, *<BackSpace>* just deletes the character immediately to the left of the current cursor position.)

If you leave BRANDS™ program B_INPUT by abnormal means (for example, by *<Ctrl-Break>*), no decision variable changes (since the last update) will be permanently written to disk. During a lengthy session of decision variable changes, you may wish to return to the main menu and execute an **Immediate Update of Decision Variable and Marketing Research Files** action occasionally to force an immediate update of all decision variables. Then, if the machine goes down for any reason, all changes to that point would have been permanently saved to disk.

The decision variable change screens consist of two general instruction screens and five decision variable change screens. These screens are arranged in a prescribed order. By pressing the *<PgUp>* or *<PgDn>* keys, you can move from one screen to the next in the prescribed order.

The prescribed order of the decision variable change screens in B_INPUT is as follows:

Screen	Screen Contents
1	Decision Variables Change Screen #1, Product 1 Marketing Variables
2	Decision Variables Change Screen #2, "Other" Product 1 Variables
3	Decision Variables Change Screen #3, Product 2 Marketing Variables
4	Decision Variables Change Screen #4, "Other" Product 2 Variables
5	Decision Variables Change Screen #5, Sales Force Variables

"Other" variables refer to research and development spending and reformulation requests. In general, "other" variables include all of those product-related decision variables that do not involve regionally-specific things.

Actually, it is possible to skip to any of the decision variable change screens at any time by using special *<Alt>* key combinations. For example, by pressing the *<Alt>* key and the *<5>* key simultaneously (hold *<Alt>* down and press *<5>* simultaneously while continuing to hold *<Alt>* down), you will immediately skip to decision variables change screen #5. The full skipping possibilities are listed below:

By Pressing These Keys	You Immediately Skip To Decision Variables Change Screen
<Alt-1>	1
<Alt-2>	2
<Alt-3>	3
<Alt-4>	4
<Alt-5>	5

By pressing *<Enter>* or any other cursor control key, you automatically move to the next data element on the screen. By pressing *<Esc>*, you will leave the decision variables change operation and return to the main menu.

After exiting B_INPUT, current values of decision variables are automatically written to file DVn.DAT (where "n" is your firm number). If you have changed your test marketing decision variables, then the current values of the test marketing decision variables are automatically written to file DVTESTn.DAT, where "n" is your firm number. These ASCII-text files may be printed or displayed on your screen.

Pre-Ordering Marketing Research Studies

Marketing research studies may be pre-ordered using program B_INPUT. Pre-ordering means that you request a marketing research study at the same time that you use B_INPUT to record your decision variable changes. Pre-ordered marketing research studies are executed immediately after the subsequent game run, so they will reflect the current quarter situation at the time the pre-ordered marketing research studies are executed. (Marketing research studies reflect the market conditions existing at the end of the just-completed game run.) When pre-ordering marketing research studies, all necessary marketing research study parameters and specifications are recorded by the B_INPUT program. These are used later during the actual execution of the marketing research studies. All marketing research studies may be pre-ordered via the B_INPUT program.

Marketing research studies may be temporarily or permanently pre-ordered. A temporary marketing research request will be executed only once, after the next quarter. Then, such temporary marketing research requests will be automatically canceled (turned-off). A permanent marketing research request will be executed repeatedly (after each subsequent quarter), until it is formally canceled. Be careful with the use of permanent marketing research study pre-orders.

After selecting **Process Marketing Research Study Pre-Order Requests** from B_INPUT's main menu, the marketing research sub-menu will appear. To select a particular marketing research study, use the cursor keys to locate the study of interest. Then, by pressing one of the keys indicated at the bottom of this screen, the appropriate pre-order activity will be processed:

- *<A>* for **Display All** results in the current status of all marketing research study pre-orders being displayed on the screen.

- *<C>* for **Cancel** results in this marketing research study pre-order being canceled.

- *<D>* for **Display** results in the current status of this marketing research study pre-order being displayed on the screen.

- *<P>* for **Permanent** results in the marketing research study being permanently pre-ordered.

- *<T>* for **Temporary** results in the marketing research study being temporarily pre-ordered.

- **<Esc>** results in marketing research study pre-orders being terminated. Program control passes back to the main B_INPUT program menu.

Some marketing research selections will lead you to infinite loops where you will be continually prompted to input more marketing research requests. To terminate such infinite loops, press **<Esc>** at the prompt. With regard to marketing research pre-ordering, program B_INPUT produces two DOS files, one that is viewable through normal DOS commands and one that is not. File PREMRSn.DAT, where "n" refers to a firm number (e.g., file PREMRS4.DAT for firm 4), is an ASCII-text file that records the current status of all marketing research study pre-orders. To display this file, type (in small or capital letters):

TYPE PREMRS4.DAT

for firm 4, for example. To copy this file to your printer (again, assuming that your are firm 4), type (in small or capital letters):

COPY PREMRS4.DAT LPT1:

assuming that your printer is a parallel printer connected to parallel port #1. B_INPUT also produces another file, PREMRSn.BIN (e.g., file PREMRS4.BIN for firm 4), which is binary in form. This file cannot be displayed at the screen or printed.

Pre-Ordering Test Marketing Experiments in B_INPUT

When using B_INPUT, you pre-order test marketing experiments just like all other marketing research studies. To pre-order Marketing Research Study #20, you must normally complete both of the following steps:

---

(1) Pre-order Marketing Research Study #20 for the desired market region(s) from within the "Process Marketing Research Study Pre-Order Requests" sub-menu in B_INPUT. When entering your test marketing pre-order requests, you will be asked to provide the length (the number of quarters) of each test marketing experiment. You may pre-order test marketing experiments at any time, before or after Step (2) below.

---

(2) From the main menu in B_INPUT, select item "Change Decision Variables For Test Marketing Experiment" and then make any decision variable changes that are to be in effect throughout the test marketing period. Decision variable changes made within the "Change Decision Variables For Test Marketing Experiment" sub-menu are only relevant for test marketing experiments; these changes have nothing to do with your normal BRANDS™ decision variables.

> **Note: Make these test marketing decision variable changes ONLY AFTER you have made all of your normal decision variable changes. If you subsequently make normal BRANDS™ decision variable changes, you MUST RE-ENTER ALL of your test marketing decision variable changes.**

The test marketing decision variables are stored in a separate file (DVTESTn.BIN, for firm "n"). These test marketing decision variables are only processed by the BRANDS™ software when test marketing experiments are conducted.

If you only complete Step (1) above, BRANDS™ assumes that no changes in decision variables are required during test marketing experiments. If that is your intention, be sure to erase any existing BRANDS™ test marketing decision variables file (issue the command **ERASE DVTESTn.BIN**, for firm "n", at the DOS prompt). If you only complete Step (2) and do not execute Step (1), no test marketing experiment is conducted.

Contents of the BRANDS™ Disk

The files on the BRANDS™ disk have the contents and uses (where "n" refers to your firm number) shown in Table 9. Note that binary files cannot be printed, listed, or edited. However, ASCII-text files may be printed or listed. Executable files are binary in format, so they may not be printed, listed, or edited.

Of these files, only B_INPUT.EXE, DVn.BIN, DVPARAMn.BIN, INDUSTRY.DAT, and PREMRSn.BIN are required to be on the BRANDS™ participant's disk at all times. All other files are not of importance to B_INPUT.

Table 9

CONTENTS OF THE BRANDS™ DISK

File Name	Description of File Contents	File Type
B_INPUT.EXE	The executable version of the B_INPUT program. This program is used to input the decision variables changes and the marketing research pre-order requests. This program uses files DVn.BIN for input and output of decision variables, file DVPARAMn.BIN for input of some decision variable parameters and limits, DVTESTn.BIN for output of test marketing decision variables, and file PREMRSn.BIN for input and output of marketing research pre-orders.	Executable
DVn.BIN	A binary file containing the current values of all decision variables.	Binary
DVn.DAT	Current values of all decision variables.	ASCII-Text
DVPARAMn.BIN	A binary file containing some decision variable parameters and limits.	Binary
DVTESTn.BIN	A binary file containing the test marketing decision variables.	Binary
DVTESTn.DAT	Current values of all test marketing decision variables.	ASCII-Text
FRESn.DAT	Financial and operating results for the just-completed quarter.	ASCII-Text
INDUSTRY.DAT	A file containing some BRANDS™ industry parameters.	ASCII-Text
MESSAGES.DAT	A message file written out by program B_INPUT.	ASCII-Text
MRSTUDYn.DAT	Marketing research results, other than "Test Marketing," for the just-completed quarter.	ASCII-Text
PREMRSn.BIN	A binary file containing the pre-ordered marketing research requests.	Binary
PREMRSn.DAT	Current pre-ordered marketing research requests.	ASCII-Test

Printing *.DAT Files on the BRANDS™ Disk

The following instructions assume that you have a parallel printer operating through the LPT1: port (parallel printer port #1). This will be the usual setup for PCs with a single dot-matrix, letter-quality, or laser printer attached.

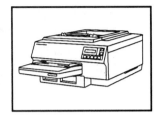

[1] Boot-up the PC. If you are using a hard disk machine, just turn the machine on. If you are using a two-disk drive machine with no hard disk, place a copy of a disk which contains the operating system in the A: drive (the left-side drive on IBM PCs) and then turn on the machine. During the boot-up phase, the operating system may ask you for the date and the time. You can just hit the *<Enter>* key twice; it is not necessary to enter the date and time. You should now be at the A> prompt.

[2] Put the BRANDS™ disk in the A: drive. If you are using a hard disk machine, make the A: drive the default drive by typing *A: .*

[3] Turn on the printer.

[4] Type (in capital or small letters),

COPY filename LPT1:

where "filename" is a particular file on the disk. For example, to print the financial results file, type (in capital or small letters),

COPY FRESn.DAT LPT1:

where "n" is your firm number.

[5] Repeat [4] as many times as necessary to obtain the desired number of copies of your firm's reports.

The files on the disk which you can print include (assuming they exist on your disk): DVn.DAT, DVTESTn.DAT, FRESn.DAT, MESSAGES.DAT, MRSTUDYn.DAT, and PREMRSn.DAT, where "n" refers to your firm number. Files DVn.BIN, DVPARAMn.BIN, DVTESTn.BIN, B_INPUT.EXE, and PREMRSn.BIN cannot be printed, since they are binary or executable files.

After a game run, the files that you will normally want to print out (if you are not provided with hard copies of them) are FRESn.DAT and MRSTUDYn.DAT, where "n" refers to your firm number.

Managing Space on the BRANDS™ Disk

The BRANDS™ participant's disk may contain 340K-350K in BRANDS™-related files. This is fairly close to the limit of 360K on a double-sided, double-density 5-1/4" disk. All files ending in *.DAT may be erased without causing any damage, since they are only incidental to the functioning of the B_INPUT program.

After printing out the *.DAT files (DVn.DAT, DVTESTn.DAT, FRESn.DAT, MRSTUDYn.DAT, and PREMRSn.DAT), they may be erased by typing the following DOS command (in capital or small letters):

*ERASE *.DAT*

Given the limited space on the BRANDS™ disk for other files, it is not a good idea to place any non-BRANDS™ files on this disk. As necessary, you may copy any BRANDS™ files from the BRANDS™ participant's disk to another disk for further processing, storage, or any other reason.

Questions, Problems, Difficulties

Any questions, problems, or difficulties that arise when using BRANDS™ program B_INPUT should be referred to your course instructor.

      If major problems arise, complete the standard BRANDS™ decision variable change forms and marketing research pre-order request forms and turn these into your course instructor at the appropriate time. Your course instructor will then arrange to have your data entered into the BRANDS™ data base prior to the next game run.

Final Reminders

Some final instructions and reminders regarding the use of BRANDS™ program B_INPUT are provided below:

✓ Only enter items for which changes are required. If no changes are required, then it is not necessary to re-enter already-existing decision variables.

✓ "Special KTM" numbers may be used when making decision variable changes. For example, 3,000,000 may be designated as 3M (where "M" means millions), 2,200,000 may be designated as 2.2M, and 23,000 may be designated as 23K or 23T (where "K" and "T" mean thousands).

✓ WHEN DROPPING A BRAND: You must also change your Advertising and Promotion expenditures to zero and reallocate your Sales Force Time Allocation from dropped brands to actively-distributed brands.

✓ Decision variable changes are only physically changed on your disk when you exit this program. Until that time, the changes only reside within the active software. To force an immediate update of all decision variable changes, go to the main BRANDS™ menu and select the **Immediate Update of Decision Variables** option.

✓ When changing the sales force time allocations, be sure to change allocations for all brands in a market region. Time allocations must sum to 100% in each region. Regional time allocation totals will flash when they do not sum to 100%.

Index